Y0-CAX-576

# PRINCIPLES OF
# Commercial Real Estate
## FINANCE

Mortgage Bankers Association of America

Dearborn™
Real Estate Education

This publication is designed to provide accurate and authoritative information in regard to the subject matter covered. It is sold with the understanding that the publisher is not engaged in rendering legal, accounting, or other professional services. If legal advice or other expert assistance is required, the services of a competent professional person should be sought.

**Senior Vice President & General Manager:** Roy Lipner
**Publisher:** Evan Butterfield
**Development Editor:** Anne Huston
**Production Manager**: Bryan Samolinski
**Senior Typesetter:** Janet Schroeder
**Creative Director:** Lucy Jenkins

© 2002 by Dearborn Financial Publishing, Inc.®

Published by Dearborn™ Real Estate Education
a division of Dearborn Financial Publishing, Inc.®
155 North Wacker Drive
Chicago, IL 60606-1719
(312) 836-4400
http://www.dearbornRE.com

Published in cooperation with the Mortgage Bankers Association of America, Inc.
Washington, D.C., © Mortgage Bankers Association of America.
Used with permission. All rights reserved.

The text of this publication, or any part thereof, may not be reproduced in any manner whatsoever without permission in writing from the publisher.

Printed in the United States of America.

02    03    04    10    9    8    7    6    5    4    3    2

While our society is a service society, the meaning of the term "service" seems to be understood by all but practiced by few. To be sure, certain industries display the requirements of "good service" more than others. One billion dollar sector of our economy delivers quality service every business day. That sector is, of course, the commercial banking industry. That industry delivers service from the initiation of a developer's concept to the closing and servicing of a commercial real estate loan. All of the requirements of the principal players must be met in a professional and timely fashion or the transaction will fail.

Commercial real estate assets are continually bought, sold, developed, and redeveloped. This makes real estate investment one of the nation's most active and important business activities. There are several types of investors, all with different criteria, all with different values, all with an assortment of analytical tools. However, all have the same objective in mind: the successful acquisition, financing, holding, and/or disposition of commercial real estate within their own definition of the profit motive.

The commercial mortgage banker must be prepared to meet the significant challenges of the current market. The demands of knowledge and service are stringent, be they in loan origination, institutional coordination, documentation, underwriting, servicing, securitization, analysis or governmental interaction. These demands may originate from the investor or from the institutional lender themselves. All have a role and all require dependable response.

Change is constant and it is most evident in commercial real estate financing. In a few short years the market has soared to unexpected highs and plunged to unanticipated lows. Tax law changes have affected investment real estate dramatically. Deregulation of savings and loans and interstate banking have seen tremendous growth of commercial mortgage-backed securities (CMBS). The CMBS secondary market size exceeds $100 billion and is growing at an accelerating rate per year. Such an industry demands service, and that requirement must be met by people trained to meet the challenges of the changing industry that contributes so much to our standard of living.

A final consideration in this fascinating world of commercial real estate finance is the increasing demand for compliance by government. In years past, the investor might investigate the price of a property and the cost to develop it, followed by the financing process and closing. Today, the first question to be addressed is: "Can the developer use the property for his or her intended purpose?" This means, can the property meet the requirements of a master plan, is the zoning appropriate, are there environmental issues to be considered, and will remediation or mitigation be a factor? What density may be applied for improvements, and what restrictions might the developer face? These and many more issues are now part of the requirements of governmental compliance and they must be met with the assistance and expertise of commercial mortgage bankers as they provide service to both borrower and lender.

Welcome to the exciting realm of commercial real estate financing. It is not an easy path you have chosen but it is rewarding and worthwhile for those with dedication and stamina.

Herbert S. Fecker Jr., CCIM

# Participants in Commercial Real Estate Transactions

1

## learning objectives

*Upon completion of this chapter, you should be able to*

- identify the processes managed by developers;

- recognize the responsibilities of mortgage bankers;

- list items contained in loan submissions; and

- specify the tasks handled by lenders.

## ■ Introduction

Commercial real estate finance occupies a unique niche among American financial service industries. It is not a business that generally receives much public attention, yet the buildings financed by commercial mortgage bankers are located in cities and towns all across the country. This business does not employ large numbers of people, yet commercial mortgage bankers arrange billions of dollars of real estate financing every year. It is a transaction-oriented venture with a focus on the next deal.

This chapter looks at the various participants in commercial real estate transactions. Specifically, we focus on the roles of the developer, the mortgage banker, and the lender. Developers control the development scenario. They prepare the raw land for building sites or rehabilitate existing buildings. Mortgage bankers originate, sell, and/or service loans served by mortgages on real property. Their clients are real estate owners and lenders. The term *lender* applies to any institution or company engaged in the process of funding commercial real estate loans.

## ■ The Developer

Developers are entrepreneurs. Like symphony conductors, they must control the varied forces in the development scenario, always within a personal conception of how to bring these forces together to create a development that, upon completion, is worth more than the cost of creating it.

It is likely that developers and their organizations have some depth of knowledge in the areas of construction, leasing, management, and sales. Depending on the size of a particular organization, there may be in-house planning, legal and financing skills as well. However, unless there is a constant high volume of development, it is probably more cost-effective for developers to contract with professionals in the marketplace to handle site planning and architecture, legal issues, and mortgage financing.

### Determining a Need

In one sense, real estate is like any other product: Unless it fills a need, there can be no assurance of its success. Development potential can be researched through professional market surveys. However, it is more likely that developers will sense, based on in-depth local knowledge, where the opportunities are and then engage a market analyst to verify their hunches. In most markets, unmet needs are quickly filled by competitors.

Three scenarios by which needs are determined include the following:

1. A dynamic economy, with continual growth in jobs and population, can spur new development of a speculative nature, such as rental and condominium apartments, warehouse and distribution facilities, retail centers, office buildings, and lodging facilities.
2. A tenant wanting to expand asks for proposals.
3. A combination of speculative development and specific tenant expansion.

The assumptions and challenges of financing these three scenarios are quite different, and mortgage bankers can work with developers to establish the likely financing available for each of these situations.

### Testing Economic Feasibility

Once a development need has been determined, the developers work on many fronts simultaneously to create a series of models for testing the economic feasibility of the proposed response to the need. Various sites are identified and analyzed for

- suitability;
- cost; and
- ability to accommodate the proposed improvements.

In this process, the developers solicit, manage, and ultimately rely on input from planners, architects, lawyers, tenant representatives, contractors, and mortgage bankers. The project is outlined on paper in sufficient detail to develop capital and income budgets, as well as to assess risk.

Mortgage bankers help estimate how much of the costs can be financed through term debt, providing developers with estimates of the terms of such debt. This enables developers to determine how much equity will be required and what the economic return on that equity will be. At this point, a decision must be made about investing the equity money and seeking partners for all or part of it. Each developer's own experience, liquidity, and knowledge of equity investors' expectations are critical in deciding whether to risk more money on the project. Frequently, mortgage bankers can determine projections to help developers attract equity funds.

During this process, leasing and money markets can change for the worse and major tenants can disappear. For example, the approval process for one shopping center in Connecticut took nine years. Generally, developers who are able to work effectively—either personally or through professionals—with municipal, state, and federal planning professionals will be more successful than those who try to push the envelope too far.

It is possible that the secured approvals do not permit the scope of the development that was initially planned. When this happens, the developers must update their economic models and conduct new feasibility studies before making another decision. Again, mortgage bankers can help by supplying current data in terms of lender guidelines, rates, and terms. Once the necessary approvals are received, the developers need a loan commitment to provide the funds for land acquisition and development.

### Constructing

Developers should know local construction costs and competent contractors. Timely completion of cost-efficient construction is always a priority after the long approval process. Tenants will be anxious to take occupancy, and, once the land is purchased and a construction loan closed, the interest meter is running without any income being generated. Nothing happens until the property is completed: No tenants can move in, the permanent loan cannot close, and some approvals may even lapse. Experienced contractors in commercial construction, with solid records of on-time completion, can save hundreds of thousands of dollars in last-minute problems.

### Leasing

Depending on the property type and nature of the leasing challenge, developers may choose to handle the leasing in-house. For properties other than apartments (retail leasing in particular), leasing can be a specialized skill. It is important for developers to consider engaging experienced brokers to complete the leasing issues. Most lenders want to approve major leases.

An *estoppel agreement* is a written statement setting forth that certain facts cannot be later repudiated.

Economic rent is one factor in the leasing equation. The cost of the landlord's work to build out the tenant spaces, the length of the lease and *go-dark*, and cancellation provisions are also critical points that must be negotiated. Tenants want their leases recognized in the event of a foreclosure. Lenders want estoppel agreements for all major leases. Mortgage bankers can help developers identify lease provisions that are critical to the lender.

### *Managing the Project*

At the heart of this complex process is the entrepreneurial developer. The successful entrepreneur is also an effective manager and, where possible, a team player. Throughout the development process, there are individuals and groups with differing agendas. Dealing effectively with varied viewpoints and bias tests the mettle and patience of a developer. Experienced developers are familiar with the sometimes opposing agendas of community groups, zoning boards, tenants, contractors, brokers, and lenders.

Mortgage bankers who are able to establish a rapport with developers work closely with them from time to time during the process. Mortgage bankers can be a valuable sounding board for developers as the feasibility of the project is tested again and again during the planning, permit, construction, and leasing phases.

Real estate development is a difficult profession at best. The risks are ever present, and many projects are never completed, resulting in substantial sums of money lost. Developers who listen carefully and understand the requirements of approval authorities, tenants and lenders—and who can bring forth developments that satisfy all requirements—will enjoy great success.

## ■ The Mortgage Banker

Mortgage banking is a service profession. Mortgage bankers have two sets of clients: real estate owners and lenders. For the real estate owners (the developers), mortgage bankers identify and negotiate term debt financing. For the lenders, mortgage bankers produce new business that meets their lending guidelines.

In addition, mortgage bankers have intimate knowledge of local real estate markets, and, therefore, can offer national lenders professional eyes and ears in a particular metropolitan area. This priceless knowledge is cost-effective for lenders because the volume of business in any one city may not justify a local representative in that city.

As payment for producing a mortgage commitment and closing for a borrower, mortgage bankers receive a mortgage banking fee, sometimes expressed as a percentage of the loan amount. This fee is typically paid at the loan closing. The origination of commercial real estate loans is more fully discussed in Chapter 3.

In addition, mortgage bankers sometimes service loans for the institutional lenders they represent. Servicing involves collecting loan payments, paying taxes and insurance, regularly inspecting the property securing the loan, handling delinquencies, and assisting the lender in any loan workouts or foreclosures. For these activities, the lender allows a small percentage of the interest collected to remain with the mortgage banker as compensation for the servicing.

A mortgage banker might have the right to represent a lender exclusively or co-exclusively with another mortgage banker in a given region. The region is usually a state, but it can be several states for some smaller lenders. Other lenders do not have exclusive correspondents and will consider new loan proposals from all qualified mortgage bankers. For these lenders, mortgage bankers act as brokers and are paid a mortgage brokerage fee by the borrower at closing.

In carrying out these services, mortgage bankers are sometimes said to *wear two hats*—that is, represent both the developer and the lender— role that can sometimes cause conflicts. However, if the mortgage banker manages to keep the transaction in perspective—to ensure that the requirements of both sides are being met—there should be little anxiety. It is sometimes better to withdraw a case from one lender and shift it to another if the transaction does not seem to be headed smoothly down the road to approval. These situations can be minimized if the mortgage banker does his or her homework on the lender's guidelines and has preliminary discussions with the lender *before* submitting the application. Now we look at the responsibilities specific to the commercial real estate mortgage banker.

## *Prospecting for Clients*

Before originating any loans, mortgage bankers should be up to speed on the types of loans that lenders are considering. Frequent communication by phone, fax, seminars, and visits to the home office can keep the mortgage banker's files updated for each lender represented.

Savvy mortgage bankers keep separate files for each lender's loan requirements. If possible, these files should include examples of recent loans made by the lender, so that the established lending parameters are clear. Unless mortgage bankers know the loan products a lender has on the shelf and is willing to offer to qualified borrowers, they will find that prospecting for clients is difficult and inefficient.

In contacting prospective clients, credibility, knowledge, and professional skills are important. As in most businesses, actions speak louder than words. Therefore, in prospecting for new clients, mortgage bankers should present a client list and good summaries of recent business closed and business in the approval pipeline. They also should demonstrate their knowledge of the development process, the current state of the immediate marketplace, and current lender preferences and guidelines.

Mortgage bankers do have competition, and they should know their own strengths and weaknesses, as well as those of the competition, so that they can present their unique competitive advantages to their clients. In discussing competitive advantage, it is best to avoid negative comments about competitors. It is better for mortgage bankers to address their own strengths, particularly those that are weaknesses in the competition. Developers will get the message. As we have already discussed, development is hard work. Mortgage bankers who are more than order takers, who are looking to perform beyond just getting a signed application and who are willing to work hard right alongside the borrowers, always make a positive impression. Novice mortgage bankers sometimes fail to realize that it may be several months after the initial contact before an application is taken.

## *Originating Loans*

Loans are originated through many sources. Those below are by no means all-inclusive, but represent the most likely sources based on industry experience:

■ Commercial brokers
■ Lenders

■ Local attorneys

■ Existing clients

■ Clients of competitors

■ Out-of-town developers

Acquisition loans may be referred to mortgage bankers through the commercial broker handling the sale. Lenders may refer business to mortgage bankers when they receive applications that do not meet their guidelines. Local attorneys representing out-of-town or out-of-state buyers or developers may make introductions.

### Securing an Engagement Letter

In discussing a proposed development with a prospective client, mortgage bankers should gather as much information as possible about the development and ask as many questions as necessary to gain a firm grasp of it. Mortgage bankers should give the client an idea of whether they believe there is an opportunity to secure a commitment from a lender.

After intense study and discussions with prospective lenders, the mortgage banker should draw up an engagement letter quickly and present it to the client for review and, hopefully, signature. It should describe the loan the mortgage banker will attempt to secure, its terms, the timing of approval, and the mortgage banker's compensation for the loan. The letter should also include a list of lending institutions that the mortgage banker has the exclusive right to approach. This is important, as no one—not the lender, the borrower, or the mortgage banker—wants the loan offered to the lender from more than one source, as serious conflicts could result.

### Developing a Loan Application

During the negotiations surrounding the engagement letter and the loan application, mortgage bankers must maintain thoughtful and frequent communication with clients. Because the engagement letter is not likely to be accompanied by a good faith deposit, it is subject to being withdrawn by the borrower at any time. Therefore, mortgage bankers should try to develop the application as quickly as possible. The timing of securing the application varies from lender to lender. The communication of preliminary data, through a preliminary submission, is usually necessary to assist the lender in determining whether it will consider an application. Because an application to a lender carries with it a good faith deposit in accordance with lender requirements, mortgage bankers are more in control of the transaction after the application is signed.

Some lenders want the mortgage banker to prepare the application; other lenders prepare their own. More lenders today are issuing applications which, while lengthy, also serve as a commitment if the loan is approved. They contain all the terms and general conditions of the loan. While these applications can be intimidating, they provide an opportunity for mortgage bankers to work out any kinks in the transaction at an early stage. After the loan is approved, the lender writes a letter stating that the loan has been approved in accordance with the application, which is then attached to, and becomes part of, the approval terms.

### Developing a Loan Submission

Much has been written about loan submissions. Most lenders have checklists and examples of what is required in a loan submission.

The following is a list of items usually contained in loan submissions:

- The proposed loan terms, as found in the loan application
- A thorough description of the neighborhood, area, city, and region in which the property is located, including such items as a site plan, city maps, strip maps, aerial photographs, demographic studies, and market surveys.
- A complete description of the improvements, including outline specifications, basic architectural drawings, and a rendering of the exterior.
- Financial and biographical information on the borrower(s), sufficient to indicate the ability to complete the property, including profiles and photographs of the borrower's past accomplishments and experience with similar properties.
- A summary of capital costs, highlighting total costs, anticipated financing, and required equity.
- A projection of rental income and operating costs, including real estate taxes, for the first complete year of the property's operation.
- A seven to ten year discounted cash flow (DCF) model of income and expense, including a reversion analysis with all identified assumptions computed for three or four different discount rates. [Note that most lenders will require an independent appraisal. Mortgage bankers should understand current appraisal practices for DCF analysis. Software programs that make DCF analysis easier are available. In all likelihood, the lender will rely on the DCF analysis of the appraiser in testing loan-to-value requirements. The mortgage banker's DCF is a dry run for the formal appraisal. If the mortgage banker fails to do this analysis carefully, it could result in a smaller loan than required, which might seriously jeopardize the relationship with the client.]
- Materials that support the DCF assumptions, such as comparable rents and sales and, when possible, comparable operating costs and real estate taxes from the mortgage banker's files.
- Copies of major leases, along with succinct one-page or two-page summaries of the major terms of these leases, prepared by the mortgage bankers to help the lender determine suitability.
- A statement from the chief operating officer or other executive of the mortgage banking firm, certifying the information in the submission and recommending the loan for approval.

*Discounted Cash Flow Analysis:* Method of applying an appropriate discount to cash to be received in the future to arrive at the present value of those future earnings.

Mortgage bankers should attempt to organize the submission material in a meaningful, logical fashion, keeping in mind that the purpose of the submission is to convince the lender to invest in the property. Through the submissions, mortgage bankers and their clients must present a winning case for this investment.

From time to time, the mortgage banker should step back and examine submissions from the perspective of disinterested investors. Potential investors are being asked to part with some of their money. "Why is this a good investment?" should be in the mortgage banker's mind as every page of the loan submission is written.

### *Underwriting a Loan*

After a lender receives a submission, there is much discussion among the parties involved—lender, mortgage banker, and developer—to identify the questions and lease terms that require negotiation. An environmental report is ordered and its findings considered. Any programs for remediation have to be negotiated. If the loan is for refinancing older property, an engineering report is ordered and any deficiencies must be resolved before closing. Finally, an appraisal is ordered and, assuming everything else has been resolved, the appraised value will set the upper limit of the loan amount. During the underwriting process, mortgage bankers act as *go-betweens*, explaining lender concerns to clients and securing answers to lender questions quickly.

### *Securing a Loan Commitment*

The delivery of the commitment by the mortgage banker to the client should always be in person. Because the client will probably have questions, the mortgage banker must be prepared to answer them effectively.

The acceptance of a commitment by the client sets the closing process in motion. The lender's counsel takes over and begins working directly with the client's counsel. Frequently, the lender has a closing paraprofessional whose job it is to keep the whole process on track. Mortgage bankers need to work closely with the client's counsel and lender's representative to make sure the process is proceeding smoothly and to interject themselves into the equation if significant business points arise. There are many details to handle during the closing process. Mortgage bankers must see to it that these details are taken care of and that the lender's commitment requirements are met.

### *Managing the Closing and Post Closing*

By the time a loan gets to closing, the process has, without a doubt, taken many months. Frequently, it takes well over a year from the date the first letter is placed in a client's file to the closing date. At the closing, mortgage bankers receive compensation for all their efforts in counseling borrowers during the development process, in assisting borrowers with pro formas, in preparing preliminary submissions to lenders, and in developing applications, commitments, and closings.

As soon as possible after the closing, the mortgage banker should set up the servicing files, if they will service the loan. Ordinarily, the lender's attorney supplies the mortgage banker with a complete set of the closing documents, so that the loan covenants can be enforced on behalf of the lender. It is wise to involve the servicing staff toward the end of the closing process, so that they can be fully familiar with the loan requirements and covenants that will be monitored monthly after the loan is closed. Commercial loan servicing is more fully described in Chapter 6.

## ■ The Lender

Without the lender, of course, none of the bills can be paid. Commercial real estate lenders might be insurance companies, savings and loan associations, mutual savings banks, commercial banks, pension funds, credit companies, real estate investment trusts, and conduits who bundle packages of loans for sale to private investors or for securitization in the form of mortgage-backed securities. As we will discuss in Chapter 2, each type of lender has its own motivation for investing in commercial real estate. For every lender, there is a different source of funds from which to lend, and there are different costs of the money.

Examples of sources of funds include the following:

- Demand deposits
- Passbook savings deposits
- Certificates of deposit
- Reserves for future life-insurance obligations
- Pension deposits
- Private investment funds on Wall Street

For all these funds, the lender pays a return to the depositor, either at set intervals or at some point in the future. What a lender has to do to stay profitable is to invest these funds at a return that will pay the lender's required interest on the deposits being invested, the lender's overhead, and a reasonable provision for losses, with something left over for profit at the end of the year. This money-mix and its yield requirements determine the broad outlines of the lending programs offered by the lender.

It is important for mortgage bankers to understand the source and cost of the lender's funds. Borrowers need not understand this in-depth, but mortgage bankers should be able to explain the derivation of a lender's programs. Through this understanding, mortgage bankers can carefully determine which loan proposals represent the best opportunities for which lenders.

### Understanding Lender Preferences

Lenders tend to develop preferences and focus on certain lending specialties. Some lenders are real estate oriented, while others are only interested in properties which are net leased to one or more credit tenants. Some prefer only one type of loan, such as loans for regional shopping centers or downtown business hotels. Mortgage bankers who attempt to "put a square peg in a round hole" by submitting loan types which do not match a lender's preferences are operating inefficiently.

### Following Lender Underwriting Practices

In evaluating loans, lenders review all items in an appraisal. Lenders' staff have elaborate spreadsheets of all similar loans approved, and they analyze each loan submitted alongside similar loans that have already been approved. Key financial ratios—such as loan-to-value (LTV), loan-to-gross income, break-even occupancy, value and loan per square foot, coverage of debt service from net income, ratios of major tenant income to total income, and percentage of tenant turnover during the loan term—are taken into account. Many of these key ratios are used in the preliminary review outlined above, to establish the basic loan parameters of amount, term, and pricing. This terminology is more fully addressed in Chapter 5.

### Developing a Loan Commitment

The loan commitment is a binding contract to fund the loan. If the loan does not fund for reasons that are not the fault of the lender, the borrower forfeits a significant good faith deposit. Commitments (or combination application/commitment) can consist of several pages, and define, in somewhat condensed legal language, the terms and conditions of the loan documents.

Loan commitments require acceptance within a stated period of time. They can be for funding upon completion of the property (for new construction), or they can be for refinancing on a recently completed or older property. For future funding agreements, mortgage bankers will be involved in construction inspections and completion inspections, conducted by professional engineers approved by the lender, in order to be sure the project is completed in a timely fashion.

### Reviewing Leases

Lenders' in-house counsel reviews leases and may request changes in lease terms to satisfy lender requirements. Lenders are particularly concerned that lease income continues unabated. At times, this is in conflict with tenant objectives. In such cases, the borrowers' counsel must skillfully negotiate lease amendments that satisfy most of the lender's requirements, yet still protect tenant interests.

### Servicing the Loan

Mortgage bankers perform their servicing duties in accordance with each lender's servicing agreement. In addition, they conduct an annual economic review of the property's performance. This review is a requirement in most lenders' mortgage documents. It calls for annual statements of income and expense for the property. In recent years, it has become much more of a priority to lenders because it provides an early warning of problem accounts and enables a lender to manage loan portfolios more effectively. Mortgage bankers should realize this priority and impress upon their clients that complete reporting fosters good relationships with lenders. In addition, meeting with a client to discuss annual operating statements provides an opportunity for mortgage bankers to discuss future business with the client.

## ■ Summary

As we have discussed, developers control the development transaction. They are faced with many challenging variables. Mortgage bankers assist the developer by helping to estimate how much of the cost of the development can be financed through term debt. This enables the developer to determine how much equity will be required and what the economic return on that equity will be.

During the development process, both mortgage bankers and lenders play a key role. Lenders rely on mortgage bankers to secure quality loan applications, assist in completing loan transactions, and assist in servicing loans. Mortgage bankers rely on lenders to provide timely feedback on lending programs and changes in policy and practices. Borrowers rely on both mortgage bankers and lenders to deliver commitments and closings on a timely and economically sound basis, in accordance with terms promised earlier. None of these parties can operate in a vacuum.

# ■ Chapter 1 Review Questions

1. A market analysis is a tool used by developers to verify their hunches.

   a. True

   b. False

2. When a developer is testing the economic feasibility of a proposed development, various sites are analyzed for all of the following EXCEPT

   a. cost.

   b. need.

   c. suitability.

   d. ability to accommodate the proposed improvements.

3. At the closing, mortgage bankers get paid for all of the following efforts EXCEPT

   a. servicing the loan.

   b. assisting borrowers with pro formas.

   c. preparing preliminary submissions to lenders.

   d. developing applications, commitments, and closings.

   e. counseling borrowers during the development process.

4. Check six common tasks performed by mortgage bankers.

   _____ Originating loans

   _____ Reviewing leases

   _____ Underwriting loans

   _____ Securing a loan commitment

   _____ Developing a loan application

   _____ Securing an engagement letter

   _____ Managing a closing/postclosing

   _____ Identifying a development need

5. Which item supports the discounted cash flow (DCF) assumptions made in loan submissions?

   a. Projection of rental income

   b. Comparable rents and sales

   c. Comparable lease agreements

   d. Projection of operating costs

6. Check items commonly contained in loan submissions.

   _____ Proposed loan terms

   _____ A summary of capital costs

   _____ An assessment of the current economy

   _____ A complete description of improvements

   _____ Financial and biographical information on borrowers

   _____ A thorough description of the neighborhood, area, city, and region in which the property is located

7. Which is NOT a key financial ratio used by lenders to analyze loans?

   a. Loan-to-value (LTV)

   b. Loan-to-gross income

   c. Discounted cash flow

   d. Break-even occupancy

   e. Value and loan per square foot

8. Lenders provide the money for development projects. All of the following are common sources of funds EXCEPT

   a. demand deposits.

   b. passbook savings.

   c. certificates of deposit.

   d. pension deposits.

   e. real estate sales.

# Commercial Real Estate Investors

## learning objectives

*Upon completion of this chapter, you should be able to*

- name the primary investors in the commercial real estate market;

- recognize the investment preferences of investors;

- identify factors that influence investment value;

- list components of the four-step investment analysis decision model; and

- describe the fundamental concepts used to estimate property value.

## ◼ Introduction

As discussed in Chapter 1, the mortgage banker makes a significant judgment concerning the maximum amount of financing that a particular property can sustain. That amount is balanced against loan interest rates, terms, and conditions and, based on a thorough analysis of the characteristics of the project, the loan decision influences the investor who might fund the project.

This Chapter introduces the primary investors in the commercial real estate market, their investment preferences, and factors that impact their investment decisions. A four-step decision model for evaluating real estate investment proposals is presented, as well as fundamental concepts used by investors to estimate investment property values.

## ◼ Commercial Real Estate Investors

A variety of lending institutions (investors) provide funds for financing commercial real estate. Investors are motivated by the need to secure instruments that match their liabilities. The primary investors in commercial real estate loans are as follows:

- Life insurance companies
- Commercial banks
- Savings banks
- Savings and loan associations
- Pension funds
- Real estate investment trusts
- Federal credit agencies
- Credit corporations

### Life Insurance Companies

Life insurance companies are the principal investors for larger commercial and industrial loans. They are attracted to mortgage loans because the yield on commercial mortgages is typically higher than the yield obtained from stocks and bonds of presumably equal quality.

### Commercial Banks

Commercial banks are the major construction and development investors. Banks, being relationship-oriented, place great emphasis on the character, experience, and financial strength of the borrower.

### Savings Banks

Savings banks have been a chief source of mortgage credit since World War II, attracted by the higher yields available on the long-term market.

### Savings and Loan Associations

Savings and loan associations and savings banks became major players in the investment arena in the 1980s. Today, more than 75 percent of the nation's savings and loan associations are commercial real estate investors, offering commercial loans, joint ventures, and syndication products.

### Pension Funds

Pension funds are becoming an important source of long-term mortgage credit for commercial real estate. Over the next several years, pension funds are expected to increase the overall percentage of assets in real estate investments and move increasingly into direct investments with the assistance of outside advisors.

### Real Estate Investment Trusts

Real Estate Investment Trusts (REITs) participate in financing commercial development through a combination of equity and lending procedures. These portfolios of income producing properties are granted conduit tax treatment similar to mutual funds, as long as they do not invest in anything but real estate. REITs normally demand high yields to compensate for their acceptance of unusual borrower or project attributes.

### *Federal Credit Agencies*

Federal credit agencies are investors like the Federal Housing Administration and the Rural Housing Service. These agencies deal mainly with multifamily loans. State and local credit agencies originate multifamily housing mortgages financed through state housing agencies.

### *Credit Corporations*

Credit corporations are usually subsidiaries of major industrial corporations, which sell debt to the public and trade on the company name. They are an excellent source of interim financing. Many credit corporations finance product types that the general lending community steers clear of, such as hotels, motels, life care facilities, and mobile home parks.

## ■ Investor Preferences

Investors tend to develop preferences for particular types of loans. These investment preferences may be motivated by

- conservative attitudes regarding safety;
- aggressive attitudes influenced by the need for high yields;
- specific past experiences; and
- prejudices of those involved in the decision making.

Most investors have basic coverage requirements and frequently determine their preliminary interest in a loan by this factor.

## ■ Investment Analysis

Real estate assets are continually bought, sold, developed, and redeveloped. This makes real estate investment one of the nation's most active and important business activities. Real estate transactions can be extremely complex, however, and consistent success requires careful analysis of all aspects of the proposed transactions.

Investment analysis and decision making are at best burdensome tasks, requiring consideration of a wide range of disparate yet interwoven elements. The analytical process is greatly simplified when reduced to a consistently applied system. Often called a decision model, this system is widely used for evaluating real estate investment proposals. A decision model is not unique to real estate, however. In spite of its complexity, real estate investment analysis is not fundamentally different from decision making in other investment areas. Whatever the nature of the investment vehicle, the investment decision process remains unvarying for those schooled in modern financial analysis and consists of four steps.

### *Step 1: Estimate Expected Benefits*

Investment assets are desired purely for the benefits the ownership is expected to bestow. In effect, investors purchase a set of assumptions about the ability of a property to produce income over the proposed ownership period. Because different investors make varying assumptions, there is not usually a general agreement about the investment merits of most properties.

### Step 2:  Adjust for Timing Differences Associated with Investment Alternatives

As a general rule, benefits are more highly prized the earlier they are expected to be received. The general preference for more immediate rather than delayed receipt is often called "time preference for money" and requires that those benefits which are expected only after a waiting period be adjusted by a process called discounting.

### Step 3:  Adjust for Differences in Perceived Risk Associated with Investment Alternatives

Just as investors are not indifferent to the timing of expected benefits, neither are they indifferent to the degree of certainty with which expectations are held. Risk is commonly interpreted as the possibility of variation between a set of assumptions about future benefits, and the benefits actually received.

### Step 4:  Rank Investment Alternatives in Terms of Relative Desirability of the Perceived Risk-Return Combinations

Attitudes toward risk differ, but rational investors seek financial return as a reward for bearing the risk associated with investment ventures. Most investors are averse to risk and insist on additional expected benefits for additional increments of perceived risk linked to an investment alternative. Differences in risk aversion levels also affect the required trade-off between risk and expected return.

## ■ Fundamental Concepts in Estimating Property Values

The investment perspective requires a slightly different view of real estate than the customary one. Investors must develop a perception of the worth of a property as an addition to a personal portfolio and compare this to an estimate of the probable price for which the asset can be acquired. Neither the worth to the individual investor (investment value) nor the price at which the property can be acquired (market value) can be determined with certainty. Rather, investors work within value ranges.

### Transaction Price

The price at which a real estate transaction has actually closed, the transaction price, is an indisputable historical fact. In the absence of interference from normal market relationships, a transaction price is the outcome of the bargaining process between a buyer and seller. Transaction price forms the basis of most estimates of the price at which a future transaction is likely to occur.

### Most Probable Selling Price

Most probable selling price is an estimate of the price at which a future transaction will most likely occur. It is a prediction of the transaction price that will emerge if a property is offered for sale under current market conditions, for a reasonable time, and at terms which are presently predominant for such properties.

### Market Value

Market value, a term generally employed by appraisers, refers to the most probable price which a property will bring in a competitive and open market, under all conditions requisite to a fair sale. The prevailing definition presumes both buyer and seller act prudently and knowledgeably, and that the price is not affected by any undue stimulus experienced by either party.

The market value concept assumes equal bargaining strength between buyer and seller, but the most probable selling price recognizes differences in the relative bargaining strength of the parties to a transaction. Market value is based on the "prudent investor" concept and places the parties in a transaction in equal bargaining positions. Most probable selling price recognizes that buyer and seller are frequently unequal in knowledge and bargaining strength, and that "undue stimulus" frequently exists.

### Subjective Value

The value of a property to the present or prospective owner, frequently called subjective value, is unique to the individual and need not be closely related to market value or most probable selling price. Subjective value represents the worth to the individual of assumed future benefits of ownership. Since there is no precise agreement on the amount of these future benefits, or on the appropriate adjustment for waiting and/or uncertainty, subjective value is necessarily limited to individual opinion.

### Investment Value

The subjective value of an investment property to a particular investor is frequently referred to as investment value. It reflects the investor's assumptions about future ability of the property to produce revenue, the likely holding period, selling price, tax consequences, risk, available financing, and all other factors that affect expected net benefits of ownership.

### Transaction Range

Investment value from the perspective of the present owner establishes the lower end of the range of possible transaction prices. Investment value from the perspective of the probable buyer determines the upper end of the range. The owner will not take less than the investment value of the property, and the prospective buyer will not pay more than the perceived investment value of the property. The actual transaction price usually falls somewhere between the two.

## ■ Estimating Investment Value

An investor who buys a particular property is, in effect, buying a set of assumptions about the ability of the property to generate cash flow over the proposed holding period, and the likely market value of the property at the end of the proposed holding period. That the physical structure is coincidental to the investment decision is sometimes difficult to grasp. Soundness of construction, distinguishing architectural features, or harmonious surroundings are relevant to the investment decision only to the extent that these factors affect the flow of benefits from ownership or control.

Of course, a prospective investor is interested in more than the amount of anticipated benefits. Equally vital concerns are when the benefits might be received and the degree of certainty with which the expectation of benefits is held. These three concerns—timing, certainty of receipt, and amount determine the relative value of investment alternatives.

### Timing

Benefits expected to be received in the far distant future add less to a property's investment value than do those whose anticipated receipt is more imminent. In general, the further into the future expected benefits lie, the lower their value today. The exact nature of the trade-off differs among investors, depending on each investor's time preference for money.

### Certainty of Receipt

Expected benefits which are viewed with a great degree of certainty are more highly valued, all things being equal, than are those which are considered more ambiguous. The exact trade-off between value and uncertainty varies with each individual investor, depending upon the degree of risk aversion.

### Amount

Financial analysts have long recognized that the value of a revenue generating asset is the revenue the asset will generate, adjusted for the time lapse between expenditure for acquisition and receipt of the anticipated revenue. Adjustment for timing differences is called discounting. The amount of the discount per time period depends on the opportunities available to earn a return on invested capital in other investments with approximately the same degree of risk, a concept frequently called the opportunity cost of capital.

## ■ Summary

Real estate investments are one of the nation's most important business activities. Investors in commercial real estate loans include life insurance companies, commercial banks, savings and loan associations, pension funds, real estate investment trusts, and credit corporations.

Real estate investors tend to have preferences for certain loan types. Reasons for these preferences vary and may include attitudes regarding safety, the need for high yields, or specific experiences of the investor.

Because of the complexity of real estate transactions, analysis is important. Investors must assess property values utilizing certain ranges within which they expect values to lie. Most investment analyses include a four-step decision model:

> Step 1: Estimate expected benefits
>
> Step 2: Adjust for timing differences of investment alternatives
>
> Step 3: Adjust for differences in perceived risk of investment alternatives
>
> Step 4: Rank alternatives in terms of relative desirability of the perceived risk/return combinations

Beginning on the next page, we have included an article from the February 1999 issue of *Mortgage Banking* magazine which provides information about investors in commercial real estate.

# INSURERS *and* CMBS

HISTORICALLY, COMMERCIAL REAL ESTATE lending has been the purview of commercial banks and insurance companies. In the 1980s, commercial lending was juiced by the savings and loan industry, but then fell by the wayside with the real estate recession later in the decade. That situation, combined with some backtracking by the banks and insurers, created a vacuum that was eventually filled by Wall Street.

Today's investment banks that are deeply involved in the conduit business saw a short-term opportunity to take advantage of a lending market that was starved for capital in the early-to mid-1990s.

"Investment banks came in and did a great job of writing capital to an illiquid market," says Sam Davis, a senior vice president at John Hancock Real Estate Finance Inc., in Boston. "But that short-term opportunity seems to be gone at this point, and real estate lending is not traditionally a business for investment banks."

After losing commercial lending market share

**Life insurers and pension funds are reclaiming market share lost to conduits in recent years. The flexibility of being able to pursue a portfolio strategy or securitization is a real advantage in today's uncertain commercial mortgage market. Several life companies and pension funds reflect on recent turmoil in the CMBS market and their plans for lending activity in 1999.**

BY STEVE BERGSMAN

ILLUSTRATION BY PHILIP BROOKER

to Wall Street, insurers—particularly the big life insurers—expect to regain lost ground now that investment banks have been pummeled by turmoil in the commercial mortgage-backed securities (CMBS) market.

"Wall Street pumped a lot of money into this market over the past three years, and they did gain market share," says Gary Kallsen, a vice president of real estate operations for Lutheran Brotherhood, a fraternal life insurance company based in Minneapolis. "For life insurance companies, the percentage of assets in mortgages fell about 16 percent. Now there has been a financial correction, and it will give it up. We probably have more staying power than conduits, and if we are patient, the market will come back to us."

The commercial mortgage-backed securities market came to life in the early 1990s with the Resolution Trust Corporation. Wall Street then picked up the game and began forming conduits to pump more liquidity into the market. In 1990, CMBS production was less than $5 billion. For 1998, production should total more than $70 billion. Most of that

> **Insurers** have been buyers of CMBS servicers and issuers, and some even formed conduits of their own. A sampling of insurers shows there will be little to no hesitation to lend. Conduit programs will go forward and where necessary, warehousing will continue.

happened before the end of August. International lending problems, particularly in Russia, sent investors scurrying for quality paper, and CMBS was one of the markets hit hard. Wall Street immediately pulled back, and its retreat has presented an opportunity to insurers.

Insurers have been buyers of CMBS, servicers and issuers, and some even formed conduits of their own. A sampling of insurers shows there will be little to no hesitation to lend. Conduit programs will go forward, and, where necessary, warehousing will continue.

A company like Principal Financial Group, whose flagship is Principal Mutual Life Insurance Company, has been in the commercial lending business for more than 50 years. Real estate is a core asset, with more than 300 employees working on that asset class alone. At present, its overall commercial loan portfolio is about $11.5 billion—a number that goes up or down slightly, depending on the market. However, over the past couple of years, Des Moines, Iowa–based Principal has averaged $2.5 billion to $3 billion in mortgage production, and that is anywhere from 400 to 500 transactions.

Despite all that loan production, the company didn't begin a securitization program until about six months ago. In a way, the timing was good—it missed the September calamity. "When the market tanked, we really didn't have

much on the books, and, in hindsight, that was pretty darn good," says Marty Cropp, director of commercial real estate at Principal. "Actually, we are just getting the whole loan production, with respect to producing securitization, under way."

Principal expects to do its first securitization by the end of the first quarter or early second-quarter 1999. "What we have learned is that we can be a long-term player in this market, and an insurance company that is willing to continue to produce whole loan mortgages for the portfolio as well as whole loan mortgages for third-party capital clients who are asking us to securitize those," Cropp says. "We added the discipline to go ahead and do conduit mortgages."

As Cropp sees it, there is a fundamental difference between a company like Principal and a Wall Street investment bank—it not only holds its own loans, but also sells a product on the other side of the insurance equation, guaranteed income contracts, or GICs. If Principal does, for example, a five-year loan, it will also do five-year GICs. "We can put those in bed together, and therefore we don't have this big interest rate risk," Cropp notes.

In other words, Principal has an asset-liability match that is different from a firm that doesn't have it; Principal must look to the public market to take them out of those loans and are subject to whatever the current market price might be.

Insurers have a lot more flexibility in regard to loans that will be securitized. Lutheran Brotherhood holds the first loss position from securitizations in its own portfolio. "We are keeping the first loss positions," explains Kallsen. "We underwrite them, and we continue to service those loans ourselves. We are both the master servicer and special servicer. The first loss position is 10 percent, so our leverage is the other 90 percent. That is the key ingredient, because other companies are unwilling or unable to do that."

Kallsen adds that, unlike Wall Street firms that have to sell their loans, the Lutheran Brotherhood doesn't. It keeps them in its portfolio and lets them mature over five or six years. In the meantime, Lutheran Brotherhood gets a 12 percent return instead of a 7 percent or 8 percent return.

Like Principal, Lutheran Brotherhood has been doing commercial lending for a long time—in its case, about 30 years—and, as Kallsen likes to say, there was never a year when it has been out of the market since it started lending. The company lends into the commercial market about $300 million to $400 million annually. "We have mortgage lending as one of our core competencies, and we stay with it," Kallsen adds.

Unlike Principal, Lutheran Brotherhood has been an active securitizer. It did its first deal back in 1996—a private placement of $65 million. In 1997, the company did about a $200 million deal, fully rated by Duff & Phelps and Moody's, and sold through Morgan Stanley. In 1998, it went back to private placement with a $190 million transaction. That last deal was in July, before the market turbulence. Since Lutheran Brotherhood feels it can be patient, it sees no need to do another deal in 1999 if the market remains volatile.

Sun Life, in Boston, didn't feel the need to put a securitization together in 1998 and doesn't know if it will in 1999, either. In 1997, it did a $153 million transaction, but kept the low investment-grade pieces and interest-only strip, valued at about $20 million. "It went very well, and financially, it was very successful," says Tim Monahan, an assistant vice president and head of the mortgage area in the investment department. Staying out of the market in 1998 seemed like a good idea. Was that because Sun Life knew something no one else did? Not really—but that doesn't mean it wasn't smart. "I would love to say we knew what would happen in the market, but that wouldn't be true," Monahan says. "We saw we needed to hold loans on our books, so we just decided not to do a securitization [last] year and to see what happens in the future."

As it turned out, its reasoning was right on. Any company with a lot of inventory got hurt pretty badly as the pricing changed quickly, making some of those loans too expensive in terms of what the market would bear.

"The issue we did in 1997 was small, which hinders liquidity a little bit," says Monahan. "Although for the time being we won't see the $2 billion securitizations. New deals will be a lot smaller, so in theory, there is less warehousing time for the mortgages." This won't necessarily entice Sun Life to do another securitization. It's perfectly comfortable keeping all its loans in its own portfolio. "But, again, if there is a chance to sell the portfolio or a piece of it and make some money, then we will do it," Monahan says.

Protective Life Corporation has been in business since 1907 and considers itself not just a multiline life insurance company, but an insurance holding company that also sells health, dental, cancer and payroll insurance, plus retirement savings plans and annuities. It treats CMBSs as an additional line of business and has done three securitizations: a Real Estate Mortgage Investment Conduit (REMIC) for $550 million in 1996, a Financial Asset Securitization Investment Trust (FASIT) for $440 million in 1997 and another FASIT in 1998 for $150 million.

"We invest for the various lines of business that the company has, and if we can profitably use the CMBS market in terms of our mortgage loan production, we do so," says Mike Prior, a vice president in investments for Protective, which is based in Birmingham, Alabama. "CMBS provides the company a little bit more diversification for the company in terms of investment profit potential," says Prior.

Protective Life's last securitization was right in the middle of market turmoil, but Prior says it was quite profitable for the company. The difference between it and the investment banks that were taking red ink on their securitizations was not that Protective could do a better job, but that it had options as to how to approach the market. "CMBS is an incremental part of our business, but is not our only business," Prior says. "A lot of the CMBS market had only one outlet for what they did, and that was basically put their mortgages into a bond format and sell it to the public, but if for some reason the public stops buying, there are limited options left in the market as it is now structured."

Protective, like other insurers, could either use its loans for its own portfolio or use some of it for CMBS. Insurers can even allocate their products to GICs they write. The point Prior makes is that everyone accumulates, but if the

> **Protective Life's** last securitization was right in the middle of market turmoil, but Prior says it was quite profitable for the company. The difference between it and the investment banks that were taking red ink on their securitizations was not that Protective could do a better job, but that it had options as to how to approach the market.

only outlet for that accumulation is securitization and there's $80 billion worth of competition at the time, then coming to market could be a problem.

Protective doesn't have its next securitization scheduled, but that doesn't mean it won't do one. Protective says it will continue to take advantage of the capital markets as opportunities arise.

Massachusetts Mutual Life Insurance Company is also taking a wait-and-see attitude. There is roughly a $20 billion overhang that is going to work its way through the system, says Ken Hargreaves, executive director of investment management at Mass Mutual. "Our guess is it is going to take three to six months, and at that point we will look and see what role everybody will take."

Taking a different tact is John Hancock, which is actively originating loans, marketing its loan products to borrowers and trying to crank up its pipeline again for its next securitization, which the company expects to happen in the first half of 1999.

The company started its conduit lending in mid-1997, and contributed $150 million worth of loans to a combined pool with Morgan Stanley and Wells Fargo in March 1998. That transaction accumulated $1.4 billion in loans.

John Hancock had a pool of loans it intended to securitize for the mid-autumn time frame, but because of the unfavorable market conditions, it decided to hold the loans.

"This was not a problem for us, and this is an important point," says Davis. "We sold this pool of loans into our general account portfolio, meaning we took on these assets which are high-quality loans and put them into our own portfolio. That differentiates life insurance companies from most other competitors in the business. John Hancock, for example, has approximately a $7 billion commercial mortgage portfolio of long-term, fixed-rate loans. We were happy to buy this pool of loans that we had originated for sale."

Davis adds, "The fact that we are going to continue to be

both a portfolio lender and a lender for securitization is what is going to allow us to survive through all sorts of market conditions that other competitors can't."

Also surviving very well, thank you, is Teachers Insurance Annuity Association–College Retirement Equities Fund, better known by its acronym, TIAA-CREF. "We are out there doing business, exactly as we were doing business six months ago when there was competition. Now there is just less competition, but there is no difference in our strategy," says Kevin Riordan, director of TIAA-CREF's commercial mortgage and real estate securities unit in New York.

While it carries the name Teachers Insurance, TIAA-CREF is basically a pension fund and has been a buyer of CMBSs ($4.5 billion purchased as of November 1998), plus it boasts its own conduit. It did its first securitization, a $260 million deal, in November 1997, and its second in October 1998, a $480 million transaction.

Echoing Cropp, Riordan notes, "As a pension fund, we are in for the long-term." Also, being a pension fund, it has a

**So far,** investment banks say they will be staying in the conduit game despite recent setbacks. Yet others say the CMBS market going forward may end up being dominated by a handful of insurance players, a couple of major banks and key financial companies like GMAC and GE Capital.

different strategy than do the insurers. TIAA-CREF does only large loans, a $50 million mortgage as opposed to a $5 million mortgage. It developed a conduit to do smaller loans that can then be aggregated. "The conduit gives me the opportunity to sort of do off-balance sheet aggregation of loans that TIAA couldn't do," says Riordan. "I use it as kind of a small-loan substitute vehicle."

To sum up TIAA-CREF's position on CMBSs, it warehouses, securitizes and buys for its own account—and that is not going to change.

Although Prudential Insurance Co. of America has been a commercial mortgage lender for 100 years, only within the past two years did it begin to hold mortgages for the purposes of securitization. Its first deal, in August, was just before the CMBS market began to deteriorate. Managed by Prudential Securities, it was a $1.2 billion transaction, of which Prudential Mortgage Capital Co., a commercial mortgage conduit, committed $370 million.

In January, Prudential Insurance combined its commercial mortgage lending groups, integrating its portfolio loan and conduit programs. The combined disciplines will operate under the existing name of Prudential Mortgage Capital Co., and will be run by David A. Twardock, who carries the title of president.

The company expects to complete one securitization with a pooling partner (to be determined) by the end of the first—possibly second—quarter, and it will still contribute to other securitizations on an ongoing basis. The theory behind contributing to other securitizations, says Twardock, is that "while branding isn't dead, the '98 turmoil contributed to the desire to treat this as a flow business. Most likely, we'll see assets inventoried for shorter periods."

Prudential Mortgage's strategy is to be able to offer a broad-range product to borrowers, says Twardock—"Portfolio product that we can hold, portfolio product that we may securitize and product that we can take directly to capital markets. This will allow us to offer the range of loan product that the borrower needs. More products mean we can complete more deals. And we have [done] and will do it through a consistent, reliable process."

Apparently, the shake-up in the CMBS markets didn't scare Prudential from going through with its securitization strategy. As Twardock asserts, the turmoil in the fall of 1998 was a disruption in the capital markets and not a credit disruption. "It brought focus to the volatility of the conduit business, and the companies that emerged will more likely be the long-term players in the business. It does not signal the end of the securitization business," he says.

In 1998, Prudential originated $4.4 billion in commercial mortgages for its portfolio and the capital markets. With its new structure, the company expects to expand total lending to more than $6 billion by 2001, with most of the increase coming in capital markets.

"There will be more of a focus on the basic bread and butter of the conduit business, and we'll see less exotic product for the time being," says Twardock. "We'll see lower leverage, more care and attention to deals and faster warehouse turnover. Portfolio lender product will be different than conduit product. Mortgage Capital fills both product needs."

There are still a lot of borrowers out there, adds Principal's Cropp. "They are a little shaken, as they should be, by the volatility in the market in August and September and the way so many of our competitors pulled out of the market. But there is still a need and desire for capital, and we are in this for the long term."

So far, investment banks say they will be staying in the conduit game despite recent setbacks. Yet others say the CMBS market going forward may end up being dominated by a handful of insurance players, a couple of major banks and key financial companies like GMAC and GE Capital.

"Investment banks have a whole different capital structure than life insurers. Investment banks don't lend for their own portfolio, as many insurers do," Mass Mutual's Hargreaves reiterates. "When insurers slowed their lending in the early 1990s, investment banks pretty much kept the religion, which was a very positive thing for real estate markets. The market just got too busy. Now there will be fewer players, and this is good for insurers." **MB**

Steve Bergsman is a freelance writer based in Mesa, Arizona.

# ■ Chapter 2 Review Questions

1. Real Estate Investment Trusts (REITS) normally demand high yields to compensate for their acceptance of unusual borrower or project attributes. Which of the following represents how they participate in commercial development?

   a. Through stocks and bonds

   b. Through multifamily housing loans

   c. Through a combination of equity and lending procedures

   d. Through a combination of joint ventures and syndication products

2. All but one of the following statements are true about credit corporations. It is FALSE that they

   a. rarely offer interim financing.

   b. are an excellent source of interim financing.

   c. sell debt to the public and trade on the company's name.

   d. finance product types that the general lending community avoids.

3. Which one of the following investors has been the major source of mortgage credit since World War II?

   a. Pension funds

   b. Savings banks

   c. Federal credit agencies

   d. Savings and loan associations

4. Which one of the following investors is expected to increase the overall percentage of assets in real estate investments and move into direct investments?

   a. Pension funds

   b. Credit corporations

   c. Federal credit agencies

   d. Real Estate Investment Trusts (REITs)

5. Future income from a property is valued higher than current income.

   a. True

   b. False

6. Investment value is based on the assumptions of the

   a. seller.

   b. buyer.

   c. mortgage banker.

   d. investor.

7. Match the description with the appropriate step in the investment decision model.

   a. Step 1

   b. Step 2

   c. Step 3

   d. Step 4

   _____ Estimate expected benefits.

   _____ Rank alternatives in terms of relative desirability.

   _____ Adjust for timing differences in perceived risk association with investment alternatives.

   _____ Adjust for differences in perceived risk association with investment alternatives.

8. The investment analysis and decision making surrounding real estate proposals are greatly simplified by utilizing a decision model.

   a. True

   b. False

9. Match the description with the appropriate concept for estimating property values.

   a. Market value

   b. Investment value

   c. Transaction price

   _____ Subjective value of an investment property to a particular investor

   _____ Outcome of the bargaining process between the buyer and seller which forms the basis of most price estimates of future transactions

   _____ Term generally used by appraisers that represents the most probable price a property will bring in a competitive and open market under all conditions requisite to a fair sale

**10.** Check all that apply to subjective value.

\_\_\_\_\_ No precise agreement on the amount of future benefits

\_\_\_\_\_ Represents value of a property to the present or a prospective owner

\_\_\_\_\_ Not unique to the individual and must be related to market value

\_\_\_\_\_ Represents the worth to the individual of assumed future benefits of ownership

\_\_\_\_\_ No precise agreement on the appropriate adjustment to value for waiting or for uncertainty

# 3

# Commercial Loan Origination

## learning objectives

*Upon completion of this chapter, you should be able to*

- identify requirements of commercial loan originators;

- note key loan processing functions;

- recognize important considerations in loan processing;

- differentiate between methods of obtaining information on the local real estate market; and

- list significant points on the loan application.

## ■ Introduction

Origination is the process of soliciting loan proposals, applications, or packages (hereafter referred to as loan applications) from developers, and submitting them to lenders for underwriting. The term *originator* as used in this Chapter applies to account or loan officers employed by mortgage bankers who submit loan applications to third party lenders for underwriting and funding. Keep in mind that, while mortgage bankers may act as originators in submitting loan applications to lenders for funding, they may also fund loans internally.

The successful loan originator should have knowledge of the following:

- Loan processing functions and procedures employed by lenders
- Organizational structure of the lender
- Local real estate market
- Loan terms generally acceptable to lenders
- Format and content of quality loan packages

**Figure 3.1** | Loan Cycle

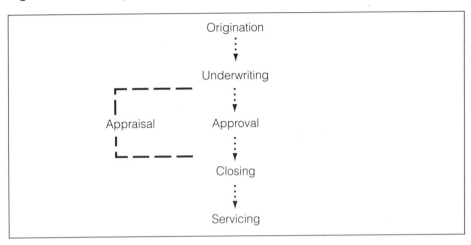

## ■ Loan Processing Functions

An originator must understand loan processing and the manner by which lenders organize all the functions required to process loans. An originator's ability to efficiently process a loan application from origination to closing depends on the organizational structures and procedures of the lender.

Given numerous departmental configurations and position titles, as well as policies and procedures, it would be difficult for an originator to fully understand every possible organizational structure. However, an originator should strive to anticipate each phase of the loan process so that timing requirements of the borrowers can be met, as borrowers are typically under significant pressure to obtain financing in order to meet sales contract deadlines or repay maturing loans. The ability of the originator to meet these requirements depends directly on the ability to understand and navigate lender operations.

Following is a description of each loan processing function, from origination through servicing, followed by examples of organizational structures.

### Origination

Origination includes soliciting loan proposals, negotiating loan terms, obtaining information from borrowers to underwrite loans, and coordinating loan closings.

### Underwriting

Underwriting consists of quantifying the credit and track records of borrowers and the feasibility of real estate projects. Underwriters apply established credit or loan policies to loan applications, which are accepted for underwriting subject to the verification of all the information collected by the originator. To facilitate underwriting, a lender may segregate credit from real estate analysis and employ credit and real estate analysts.

Credit and/or real estate analysts (often referred to as underwriters) are responsible for the following:

- Considering loan terms
- Conducting market research
- Requesting and obtaining credit and real estate information from prospective borrower(s), or from the originator
- Ordering credit reports, appraisals, environmental assessments, and engineering reports
- Preparing a detailed written analysis of the loan proposal
- Presenting the analysis to senior management

All information collected by the originator must be analyzed. It is the underwriter's responsibility to determine the risk factors and the ultimate feasibility of loan proposals.

### Approval

Once all information has been received, reviewed, and analyzed, the underwriter prepares and presents the loan package to senior management for approval. A lender typically grants lending authority to either the board of directors, loan committee, or officers, based on the size of the transaction.

An example of loan approval succession in a typical life insurance company is illustrated below:

**Level 1: Regional Manager.** No two mortgage loan department processes are the same, but typically an analyst reviews the submission and appraisal and makes a recommendation to the regional manager. The analyst or manager then recommends the mortgage to the loan committee.

**Level 2: Loan Committee—under $20 million.** Below a specified amount (for example, $10 million to $20 million), it may be customary for the head of the department plus two officers to grant approval without a committee meeting.

**Level 3: Investment Committee—$20 million to $50 million.** Above $20 million, the loan is reviewed again by an investment committee usually comprised of senior mortgage loan and fixed income professionals.

**Level 4: Board of Directors—above $50 million.** Above a certain large loan amount, say $50 million, the board of directors customarily reserves approval authority.

If the company is managing portfolios for others, there may be a portfolio committee that also approves the loan. In most companies, this approval process can be accomplished in 30 days or less.

It should be noted that regulated lenders, such as banks and savings and loans, are further limited by "loans to one borrower" regulations, which limit the lender's loan authority based on a percentage of capital and the amount of loan commitments to one borrower.

For example, a lender may be considering a loan of $10,000,000 to XYZ, L.P., but a general partner of XYZ, L.P., is also currently a general partner in other partnerships that have borrowed $40,000,000 from the lender. As a result, the total loan exposure to be considered is $50,000,000. The $50,000,000 is compared to the lender's approval hierarchy and legal lending limit (percentage of capital) to determine the approval authority and ability of the lender to fund the loan.

### Appraisal

A lender may require an appraisal prior to the presentation of the loan to its senior management, or loan approval may be given "subject to" the appraisal. In some cases, a lender may accept the borrower's appraisal (if the appraiser is a Member Appraisal Institute [MAI] and acceptable to the lender). The point at which an appraisal is required can become a key issue affecting a loan application. Depending on the project type, an appraisal can take from 60 days to 120 days for completion.

If a lender approves loans subject to appraisals, then the originator must determine how the lender addresses an appraisal which results in a lowered loan amount. If the underwriter has authority to lower the loan amount, given the approved loan-to-value (LTV) ratio, the loan can proceed on schedule. However, if a loan must be resubmitted because of a lower than approved appraisal, the loan application can be delayed.

Some lenders have appraisal departments that

- establish lists of approved appraisers;
- review appraisals submitted by third party appraisers; and
- prepare internal appraisals.

Other lenders give underwriters authority to accept and review third party appraisals.

### Closing

The loan closing is the most important part of the loan cycle, because a poorly closed loan could significantly impair a lender's legal rights. The following are needed to close a loan:

- Outside legal counsel must be selected.
- Loan documents prepared by legal counsel are reviewed.
- The terms and conditions of loan documents are negotiated.
- Loan closing checklist items are coordinated.
- Funds are disbursed.

Legal counsel should represent all parties to a loan. Lenders and borrowers have many options with respect to legal representation, and they may use outside or in-house attorneys. Also, lenders may have standardized loan documents. Absolute authority may be delegated to the attorney to institute document changes, or it may be a requirement that certain types of document changes must be submitted to senior management.

Various documents must be coordinated among the parties to a real estate transaction. Typically, the lender's attorney prepares loan documents which include the following:

- Note
- Deed of trust
- Assignment of leases and rents
- Financing statements
- Assignment of plans and specifications
- Guarantees

The borrower's attorney

- reviews the loan documents;
- orders title insurance, insured closing certificates, surveys, and engineer's or surveyor's certificates;
- obtains estoppel letters from tenants;
- provides written opinions to the lender; and
- submits other required documents.

The parties to a real estate transaction must reach mutual agreement on the terms of loan documents. The borrower's attorney reviews documents and negotiates document changes with the lender's attorney.

Once the parties have reached agreement on terms of the loan documents, and the borrower's attorney has submitted all required documents, a loan can close. Loan closing may be coordinated through loan servicing.

### Servicing

Loan servicing involves the following:

- Sending payment notices to borrowers
- Receiving and applying loan payments
- Assessing collateral
- Collection and monitoring loans

In addition, it may include finalizing loan closings. Loan servicing may be responsible for reviewing all legal documents executed among the parties as well as all checklist items.

Once loan servicing ascertains that all documents have been properly executed and received, it may then coordinate the transfer of funds from the lender to the title company. The title company then records all documents and disburses the funds in accordance with the terms of the insured closing letter.

## ■ Organizational Structure

As illustrated on the following page, there are many possible organizational structures which are used by lenders. No one structure is necessarily better. And just as there are different structural possibilities, the personnel working within these departments may have different titles and responsibilities.

**Figure 3.2** | Sample Insurance Company Organizational Structure

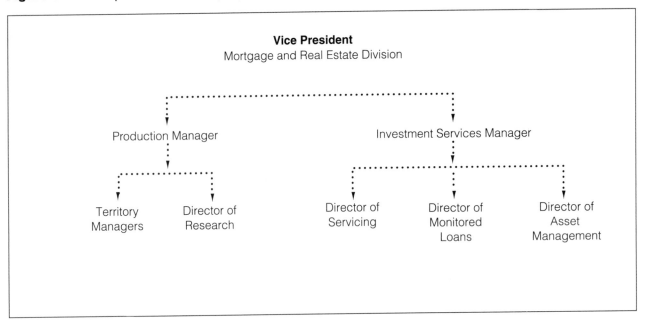

**Figure 3.3** | Sample Bank or Savings Bank Organizational Structure

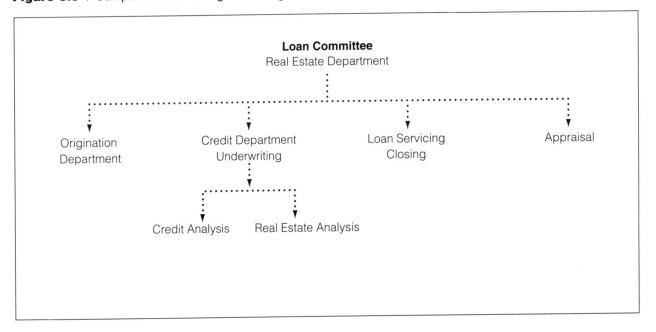

# ■ Local Real Estate Market

The efficient origination of commercial real estate loans requires knowledge of local real estate markets and an involvement in local real estate issues and participants. Some methods for obtaining information and becoming involved are discussed in the following paragraphs.

## *Touring Local Areas*

An obvious but effective way to become familiar with an area in which you would like to originate loans, as well as submarkets and types of properties, is to obtain an area map and tour the areas of interest. By touring an area, an originator can develop a list of

- future projects to be built on raw land;
- projects under construction; and
- completed projects.

There are signs on most projects identifying the names of the developer, architects, engineers, and leasing agent (broker), as well as the size of the project, names of future tenants, percentage leased, and rental rates.

## *Land and Zoning Records*

Each municipality maintains zoning maps within its real estate assessment, taxation, or land records division. The maps indicate the zoning applicable to certain areas and parcels of land. By reviewing zoning maps, the industrial, office, and residential areas can be identified. In addition, the land records division of most municipalities maintains grantor/grantee indices and property tax files that contain information on specific projects, developers, and lenders.

The following scenario illustrates the practical use of land records. For example, assume that while you are driving through an area, you pass a building and make note of the address. You call the broker assigned to the project and discover that the project is complete and 85 percent occupied. Since you are originating permanent loans, the project seems to be a good candidate.

Before calling the developer, you decide to conduct some basic research to learn more about the project. According to the land records, the project is owned by XYZ, L.P., and the land was purchased on 1/28/90 (deed book 7000, page 1000). You look up the deed book and page number, and review the deed.

The deed indicates that ABC CORP. conveyed the property to XYZ, L.P., for $2,000,000. You also note that following the deed is a copy of the deed of trust. The deed of trust indicates that Risky Bank, N.A., made a construction loan to XYZ, L.P., in the amount of $10,000,000. Also, the notice section of the deed of trust indicates that all notices are to be forwarded to Fred Blank, Vice President of Risky Bank, N.A., and George Frank of XYZ, L.P. On the last page of the deed of trust, the general partner of XYZ, L.P., Harris, Inc., executed the deed of trust.

Now that you have some understanding of the history of the project, you call Fred Blank at Risky Bank, N.A., and learn that the project is doing very well, and that the developer, Harris, Inc., is seeking a loan to refinance the project. You give the loan officer your name and number, and the lender subsequently puts you in touch with the developer.

As will be discussed later, many developers maintain brochures identifying their projects. Another way to acquire facts and figures about a developer's portfolio, without asking the developer for information, is to research the properties listed in the brochure in the land records. An alternative approach is to look up the developer's name in the grantor/grantee's index, which provides a list of instruments executed by the developer, including deeds and deeds of trust. This may be difficult, though, because most developers own projects through various partnerships.

The same type of research can be undertaken regarding a particular lender. It may be extremely difficult and time-consuming, however, because lenders typically execute numerous real estate documents and finance other types of real estate, such as residential housing.

### Industry Publications and Newspapers

These sources provide background on specific transactions, along with names of brokers, lenders, and developers. In addition to providing the originator with general and comprehensive facts about real estate markets, local newspapers sometimes provide detailed information regarding particular real estate transactions, as well as market statistics (i.e., area vacancies). These publications may have advertisements and articles on developers, lenders, projects, and other real estate professionals.

### Local Industry Associations

An originator should consider becoming a member of one or more industry associations. This provides the opportunity to meet and socialize with developers, lenders and consultants, and attend seminars and industry-specific lectures. Local industry associations also produce directories, which provide the names of member companies and officers.

### Newsletters and/or Reports of Local Real Estate Planning Boards

Many local real estate planning boards of municipalities publish newsletters containing information on zoning and other real estate matters which they have undertaken for review and/or decision. Moreover, in some jurisdictions, the planning board hearings are carried live by cable television or radio. Regardless of the medium, the information that can be obtained from planning boards includes the names of developers, engineers, projects, etc. In particular, the status of projects can be ascertained.

As an example, suppose that XYZ, L.P., has a rezoning request to be considered by the real estate planning board. The land is to be improved with a 66,000 square foot office building. The planning board has agreed to grant the developer's request to rezone the parcel from residential to office. The developer may be interested in an acquisition, development and construction (ADC) loan. If this does not lead to a loan proposal regarding the project under consideration by the planning board, perhaps the developer has other projects that need financing.

### Exploring Specific Markets

To expand knowledge of a unique submarket, the originator can study several buildings in a particular area. This can be very useful when an originator is collecting market information for specific loan proposals, or when an originator is contacting developers regarding specific projects. Developers are inclined to forward loan packages to informed originators, rather than to lenders without such knowledge.

### Local Real Estate Brokers

In addition to providing information on particular projects and submarkets, real estate brokers can be an excellent source for new loan proposals. Brokers may be involved in a number of commercial real estate transactions that require financing.

Once an originator has successfully procured a loan for a client of the real estate broker, it is likely that the broker will refer the originator to other brokers. Certainly if the transaction is successful, the broker will be inclined to provide the originator with another opportunity.

### Developer's Portfolio and Cold Calling

As already mentioned, most developers produce a brochure listing their projects. In reviewing this, an originator can obtain information on all the developer's projects without formally requesting it. Coupled with land records and other techniques, an originator can thoroughly research a developer's portfolio and produce a list by project type of potential financing opportunities. Having done the homework on the developer's portfolio, the originator can then contact the developer to ascertain financing needs.

An originator may attempt to *cold call* a developer. While this technique can sometimes be useful in isolated instances, it is generally not very successful without an introduction from a third party and/or specific information about the developer. Successful originators must distinguish themselves from other originators and cold calling does not necessarily accomplish this. Nonetheless, when carried out in conjunction with other marketing efforts, cold calling may generate leads.

### Local Chamber of Commerce

Each local Chamber of Commerce maintains company listings by industry, along with the names and phone numbers of officers. This can be useful for networking or for getting a general sense of the players in the local real estate market.

### Existing Customers and Other Developers

If you are currently employed as an originator for a lender, your existing portfolio may provide financing opportunities. Actively calling on existing customers is required to keep abreast of their financial performance and position, and secured real estate projects. In addition to obtaining financial information and monitoring collateral, actively calling on customers may lead to new business.

Your borrowers may have other projects that require financing and may also be willing to introduce you to other developers. When calling on a developer, it would certainly be appropriate to ask for referrals to other prospective borrowers.

### *Real Estate Professionals*

Engineers, appraisers, architects, and other professional consultants to the commercial real estate industry are at best an ancillary source of information, but they can provide information on developers and upcoming projects.

### *Public Offering Statements*

Should an area developer operate as a Real Estate Investment Trust (REIT) or other publicly traded entity, the public offering statements, financial statements, and disclosure statements filed with the SEC provide an originator with considerable detailed information about a developer's operations, officers, portfolio, and financial performance and position.

Publicly traded entities typically have a director of investor relations who sends quarterly and annual reports to any potential investor upon request.

### *Advertising*

The key to successful advertising is placement. Local real estate publications and the business section of local newspapers are probably the best and most cost-effective advertising mediums.

## ■ Loan Terms Acceptable to Lenders

Lenders are usually specific about the type of loans, projects, and terms that will be considered. While it should be easy to develop an understanding of the types of loan and projects acceptable to lenders, it may be more difficult to determine the specific terms and conditions under which lenders will make loans.

It is not always easy to obtain a lender's consent to specific loan terms, however. All of the terms listed above are important to the prospective borrower and lender. For example, a lender may agree to all of the terms contained within a loan application except for the interest rate.

The process of obtaining a lender's agreement to process a loan under the terms proposed may be further complicated by a lender who requires different terms based on type of loan and project. In addition, some lenders impose different terms for loan applications that involve unusual credit and/or real estate risk.

It is the originator's responsibility to confirm that a lender will accept the proposed terms prior to forwarding the loan for underwriting. Given the strength of a loan proposal, a lender may insist upon terms and conditions (e.g., personal guarantees) during underwriting that were not contemplated during the initial loan application.

It is also the originator's responsibility to inform the borrower when a lender indicates that a loan package contains unusual risk factors and there is the possibility that additional conditions may be imposed. This allows the borrower to make the decision to continue or terminate the application.

# ■ Format and Content of Loan Applications

A typical loan application includes the following basic loan terms, which are relevant to all loan applications:

**Borrower(s)**—Name of borrower (if a partnership, names of general and limited partners; if a corporation, names of shareholders).

**Guarantor(s)**—Names of entities or individuals providing guarantees.

**Purpose**—Refinance (need maturity date) or purchase (need copy of contract). If refinance, how much equity is requested beyond repayment of the existing loan?

**Loan Amount**—How much is requested?

**Rate**—Proposed rate, variable or fixed.

**Term**—Length of the loan.

**Payments**—Amortization schedule or payment constant.

**Fees**—Shown as a percentage. What is fee based on?

**Collateral**—Priority of lender's secured interest (i.e., first deed of trust), location (city, county, state) and legal description.

**Loan-to-Value**—What value is being used?  Purchase price?

**Ratio (LTV)**—Appraisal?

**Debt Coverage Ratio (DCR)**—What is the DCR and what is it based on? (projections or historical operating results)

To facilitate the underwriting process and to ensure that all of the above areas are addressed, some lenders utilize loan application forms and require borrowers to pay nonrefundable fees up front for appraisals, environmental studies, credit reports, and/or underwriting prior to underwriting a loan proposal. In such cases, the originator should

■ forward the application form to the borrower;

■ ensure that the borrower properly completes the application form; and

■ remit the signed application form with any required fees and financial information to the lender for underwriting.

In addition to an application form, lenders may also utilize standard information lists to ensure that prospective borrowers submit the necessary information to fully evaluate the feasibility of the real estate and credit of the borrower.

While it is desirable to have borrowers sign application forms, pay up-front fees and present all requisite financial information, still many borrowers submit incomplete loan packages. The burden is placed on the originator to screen and review loan packages before requiring the borrower's signature, fee payment, or submission of financial information.

# ■ Screening and Reviewing the Loan Application

The screening process includes

1. reviewing the type of loan and secured property;
2. analyzing proposed terms, inspecting the project;

3. obtaining credit reports on borrowers and principals; and
4. determining the purpose of the loan request.

A loan application should contain key information that allows the originator to answer basic questions. The idea behind screening and reviewing loan applications is that time will not be spent processing grossly incomplete loan applications.

### Important Considerations

Points 1 through 3 above are significant factors in the review process, because each could produce serious consequences if handled inadequately or improperly. The originator should always inspect the property and obtain credit reports on the prospective borrower and principals.

### Purpose of the Loan Request

Point number 4 requires thorough understanding by the originator. Borrowers need financing for two basic reasons:

1. To finance the purchase of a property
2. To refinance an existing loan

Even in the case of an acquisition, development, and construction (ADC) loan, a borrower is either purchasing land or refinancing an existing land loan. Timing is the most crucial element in all loan applications, since prospective borrowers may have entered into sales/purchase contracts or face an upcoming loan maturity date.

A typical sales contract contains feasibility periods and a specified settlement date. Prospective borrowers are likely to secure such a contract with a substantial deposit. If a borrower is refinancing and fails to secure new financing prior to maturity of the current debt obligation, the borrower is in monetary default. The lender may initiate foreclosure proceedings. Another possibility is that a developer is requesting the refinance of a delinquent loan.

The purpose of the financing must be understood because an originator could place a lender under a significant burden due to time constraints. For example, if it normally takes a lender 120 days to underwrite and close a transaction, a loan application which requires a lender to fund in 30 days would not be feasible.

### Basic Questions when Reviewing Loan Applications

Following are questions to consider when reviewing loan applications:

- Do you know the borrower, general partners, shareholders, guarantors, etc.? Can you get references from other sources?
- What is the structure and who are the owners of the borrowing entity?
- Is the loan amount too small or large relative to the borrower's other loans or the lender's loan limits?
- Are the proposed interest rate, fee, repayment terms, and maturity acceptable?

- If this is a purchase, how much is the purchase price and is the LTV ratio based on the lower of the purchase price or appraised value (if an appraisal is available)?

- When must the loan close to meet the borrower's contractual obligation? If this is a refinance, when was the property purchased? How much was the purchase price? How much is the loan to be refinanced? Is the borrower attempting to "cash out" on the refinancing and is the LTV ratio based on an appraisal? When does the existing loan mature and is it in default?

- What is the basis for the proposed DCR? Is there sufficient financial information to allow the originator to conduct a cursory review of the historical and pro forma net operating income of the proposed project? Is there sufficient financial information to initially comprehend the credit capacity of the borrowing entity, general partners, shareholders, or guarantors?

If basic questions remain unanswered, or if the borrower is unwilling to accept required loan terms, the application should be quickly and courteously denied, in writing.

An originator should also deny a loan application under the following conditions:

- The lender is not able to underwrite and close the transaction within the required time frame. Obviously, if the borrower can adjust the timing requirements, then a loan application can be continued.

- The type of loan, terms, and secured property are not feasible.

- An initial property inspection is unsatisfactory.

- Credit reports and references are unsatisfactory.

Grossly inadequate loan proposals, packages, or applications may indicate that a borrower does not have experience, expertise, or financial management. On the other hand, a complete initial loan application demonstrates a prospective borrower's sophistication. However, it would be unusual for a borrower to address every question or provide all financial data up-front with the initial loan package. As a result, the originator should always anticipate the need to request additional financial information prior to underwriting.

### *Information Required to Support a Loan Application*

Once the application has been screened and reviewed, it is necessary to confirm that the financial data submitted by the borrower is sufficient. The best approach is for the originator to obtain a list of items required by the lender (if available) and aggressively approach the borrower for all mandatory information.

While this may sound simple, it can be extremely difficult to obtain sufficient financial data from developers. The difficulty depends on several factors, including

- the quality of the borrower's management team;
- the financial records the borrower maintains;
- the borrower's willingness to disclose; and
- the confidence the borrower has in the originator.

A responsive originator who is up-front and honest about timing and loan feasibility has the best chance of obtaining necessary financial information. It helps to put yourself in the developer's shoes and ask yourself the following:

■   Would you want to provide volumes of financial data to someone who has already taken two months to conduct an initial review of a loan application, only to find out that it will take another 90 days to submit your proposal to a loan committee?

■   Would you want to provide additional information to an originator who is unsure of timing or key dates and has no idea whether or not your loan proposal is feasible?

Probably not. Therefore, an originator is more likely to obtain information if

■   loan packages are quickly screened and reviewed;

■   a commitment to a time frame for underwriting and submitting the loan to a loan committee is given to the borrower; and

■   the originator has the ability to determine if a loan package is viable.

By refusing to further process a loan application until all sufficient information has been received, an originator forces the prospective borrower to provide everything that will facilitate underwriting. This is in the developer's best interest also, because the lender's senior management can then quickly consider a loan for underwriting.

### *Loan Fees*

As mentioned previously, along with financial information, some lenders require borrowers to prepay fees for underwriting, appraisals, and engineering studies, and for preliminary hazardous waste assessments. Many times these fees are nonrefundable.

Requesting a developer to pay up-front, nonrefundable fees can be difficult, depending on the developer's confidence in the originator and the strength of the loan application. This requirement provides the originator with significant leverage and allows weak loan applications and borrowers to be weeded out.

A developer who is unwilling to pay up-front fees may not have:

■   been really prepared to commit to the loan in the event of approval;

■   confidence in the proposed loan;

■   sufficient financial data to support the loan;

■   experience in procuring loan commitments; or

■   executed a sales agreement (for the purchase of a property).

Certainly, a borrower who pays substantial up-front fees is willing to stand behind the proposal and provide financial data to support the loan application.

**Figure 3.4** | Key Time Elements in a Real Estate Sales Contract

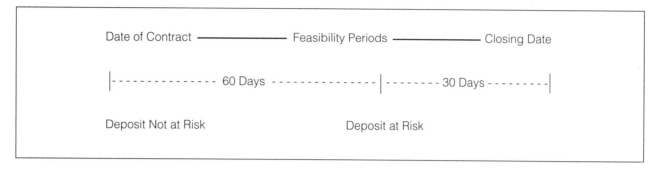

## ■ Preparing and Submitting the Loan Package

Once the loan terms have been negotiated with the prospective borrower and all required information has been received, the originator should prepare a loan package consisting of

1. a term sheet;
2. a table of contents (include all information, maps, etc.); and
3. all information obtained from the developer.

If the lender requires the prospective borrower to sign application forms, then the originator should forward the form to the borrower and ensure that it is properly completed and signed prior to submission to the lender. Any up-front fees should be collected from the borrower and submitted to the lender. Once the loan application is complete, the originator should forward it to the underwriter.

## ■ Lender Liability

There are many possible circumstances under which an applicant or borrower can make a lender liability claim. A lender can have exposure to such a claim because of misleading or improper communication with a borrower and/or negligent processing of a loan application. While this book does not provide an exhaustive discussion regarding lender liability, it is important to discuss how an originator or lender can be exposed to lender liability during origination.

Prospective borrowers are seeking a loan to either purchase or refinance property and timing is relevant in both circumstances. If a prospective borrower is under the impression that a loan is approved or will be approved, and chooses to act or not act on this belief, an originator or lender could have lender liability exposure. As a result, the key to avoiding lender liability is to make sure that both points below are adhered to:

1. understand the terms of the borrower's sales contract or the maturity date of the loan to be refinanced; and
2. communicate effectively with the borrower.

## Purchase

The simplified diagram in Figure 3.4 serves to illustrate certain key time elements relative to a typical real estate sales contract.

Going at risk on a sales contract generally means allowing a feasibility provision in a contract to expire. The expiration of a feasibility provision may put the developer's deposit at risk or may require the developer to increase a deposit.

A developer may also be subject to liquidated damages (the deposit) and a lawsuit for specific performance in the event a contract does not settle on the closing date. In addition, the developer could lose a property under contract upon the expiration of a closing date.

A developer who elects not to extend the feasibility period or closing date, under the premise that a loan will be made and/or closed on a certain date, could clearly be acting against their own best interest.

## Refinance

A lender whose loan has matured will either

- extend the loan;
- initiate legal proceedings against the borrower (or guarantors); or
- informally forbear.

A borrower could be caused harm if the lender proceeds to enforce its rights under the legal documents.

An originator should know the maturity date of a loan to be refinanced. A borrower whose lender is not currently acting on a matured loan is at risk. Borrowers who decide not to seek an extension of maturing loans may be placing themselves at risk.

## Communication

The originator must appropriately handle written communication and conversations with prospective borrowers. Written communication should always refer to a *prospective* or *proposed* loan. It may further state that the loan has not been approved until loan terms are contained within a written commitment letter.

Conversations with borrowers about the status of a loan and timing are critical. An originator should remind the borrower that they have no authority (if true) to approve or deny the loan. They should avoid offering advice to developers regarding timing elements in sales contracts or maturing loans.

Originators should provide information on the time required to process, underwrite, and close a transaction on the basis that the borrower understands that such time frames are appropriate only *if* the loan is approved.

The originator should think of the borrower-seller relationship (for a purchase) or borrower-current lender relationship (for an existing loan to be refinanced) as having separate and distinct financial and legal contexts than the borrower-originator relationship. The originator can offer advice on loan processing time frames and inform the prospective borrower of loan status. However, an originator should refer a borrower to legal counsel regarding negotiating specific terms of sales contracts or loans and should avoid conversations with any party to the borrower's sales agreement or the borrower's lender. Any time an originator has specific conversations with the borrower's seller or lender, the originator could blur the relationships among the parties.

For example, assume that you are an originator who has received a loan package from a developer. The developer outlines the transaction and provides preliminary information. Based on this information, you believe the loan to be feasible. In discussing the loan terms with the developer, you state that the loan proposal will be funded. In the meantime, the developer has a sales contract to purchase a $10,000,000 office building. Under the terms of the contract, the developer has put up a $200,000 cash deposit, which is protected by a financing feasibility period expiring in two weeks. You, as the originator, fail to read the contract and the expiration of the feasibility period. Based on your prior statement, the developer believes that there will be no problem in obtaining the loan and allows the financing feasibility period to expire. The developer is now at risk for its deposit. Obviously, if the loan is subsequently denied, the developer could lose the deposit.

If you, as the originator, had reviewed the sales contract on receipt of the loan application, you would have realized that the financing feasibility period was about to expire. Consequently, you could have told the developer the loan was not approved, and reminded the developer that the contract contains a financing feasibility period.

In this case, a letter to the developer outlining these two points would certainly have provided the originator and the lender with useful documentation and provided the borrower with information regarding the status of the loan application.

### Declining the Loan Application

Because it is likely that the majority of loan applications will not be feasible, one important responsibility of an originator is to deny loans. When an undesirable loan application is received, the originator should quickly inform the prospective borrower, in writing, that the opportunity to consider the loan application is appreciated, but the loan application has been denied. If the originator wants to develop a lending relationship with the developer, it should also be explained to the developer that future loan applications are welcome. Successfully denying loans requires quick decisions and a courteous response.

## ■ Summary

In order to be effective, an originator must be proficient in many diverse areas. From developing leads to understanding the needs of the commercial loan underwriter, the originator is a master of many trades. Negotiating skills are required to ensure that packages contain acceptable loan terms and information for underwriting. Quick action on undesirable applications and effective communication with prospective borrowers lead to success for both the originator and his or her employer.

## ■ Chapter 3 Review Questions

1. The process that requires soliciting loan proposals, negotiating loan terms, obtaining information to assess risk, and coordinating loans is called
   a. servicing.
   b. appraisal.
   c. origination.
   d. underwriting.

2. Loan originators are loan or account officers employed by mortgage bankers who submit loan packages to third party lenders for underwriting or funding.
   a. True
   b. False

3. It is the underwriter's responsibility to determine all risk factors and the ultimate feasibility of loan proposals. Check all activities that apply to the underwriting process.
   _____ Considering loan terms
   _____ Conducting market research
   _____ Performing real estate appraisals
   _____ Requesting real estate information
   _____ Quantifying credit and track records of borrowers

4. Which one of the following activities is NOT a common loan processing function?
   a. Appraisals
   b. Origination
   c. Underwriting
   d. Loan approval
   e. Loan closing
   f. Loan servicing
   g. Portfolio development

5. Lenders typically give lending authority to all the following EXCEPT
   a. officers.
   b. loan committee.
   c. internal auditors.
   d. board of directors.

6. A key issue affecting a loan application is the _____ requirement, which can take 60 to 120 days.
   a. review
   b. lending
   c. appraisal
   d. processing

7. Check three reasons why membership in an industry association is a valuable way for originators to obtain information on local real estate markets.
   _____ Membership provides credibility to the originator.
   _____ Membership provides the opportunity to attend seminars.
   _____ Membership provides the opportunity to hear industry-specific lectures.
   _____ Membership provides the opportunity to meet and socialize with developers, lenders, and consultants.

8. Sometimes information on a specific submarket is important to the originator. An effective way to develop knowledge of a specific submarket is to
   a. obtain zoning maps.
   b. call on existing borrowers.
   c. contact loan real estate brokers.
   d. study several buildings in the area.

9. The idea behind screening and reviewing loan applications is that
   a. it is required by the FDIC.
   b. it promotes standard industry practice.
   c. grossly incomplete loan applications should not be processed.
   d. grossly incomplete loan applications account for 70% of all loan applications submitted.

10. Check three significant factors to consider when reviewing a loan application.
    _____ Loan type
    _____ Property type
    _____ Proposed loan terms
    _____ Prepayment terms

# Commercial Loan Products

*Upon completion of this chapter, you should be able to*

- characterize the four basic types of commercial loans;

- recognize common underwriting considerations associated with each of the four types of commercial loans; and

- identify key aspects of a letter of credit and a forward commitment.

## ■ Introduction

This Chapter provides an overview of the four basic commercial loan products— (1) land acquisition; (2) acquisition, development, and construction (ADC); (3) mini-perm, and (4) permanent. Chapter 3 touched on the underwriting process that is used to determine risk factors that may affect the borrower's ability to repay the loan. However, the project type also has a significant implication on the underwriting of the loan. As will be presented, the repayment of a commercial real estate loan results from the underlying collateral, because the loan is repaid from the net operating income of the secured property during the term of the loan, and/or from the sale or refinance of the secured property at maturity. Therefore, the primary emphasis when underwriting the loan should be the feasibility of the real estate project.

## ■ Commercial Loan Types

Opportunities to finance commercial real estate depend on the extent to which a project is complete. Regardless of the type of commercial property (office building versus shopping center), a parcel of land is acquired or leased, a building is constructed on the acquired land, and the resulting building is ultimately leased to tenants or occupied by the owner. The building process provides financing opportunities from the time the land is acquired until the building is constructed and leased. Developers can acquire land, construct buildings, and/or acquire existing buildings.

A developer may need any of the following four types of loans:

1. Land acquisition loan
2. Acquisition, development, and construction loan (ADC)
3. Mini-perm loan
4. Permanent loan

The need for each loan type varies. For example, to induce a lender to make an ADC loan, a developer may need to obtain a forward commitment for permanent financing. Finally, a letter of credit may be required to bond on-site and off-site improvements in the development of a parcel of raw land.

*Forward Commitment* is an agreement between a buyer and seller for delivery of a specific commodity at a given time in the future, at a strike price determined at present.

## ■ Land Acquisition Loan

A land acquisition loan is a loan to finance a developer's purchase of a vacant parcel of land only—not improvements on or to the land. There are several underwriting issues associated with a land acquisition loan:

- Debt service
- Repayment of principal at maturity
- Development experience
- Land planning issues
- Zoning
- Request for an expedited loan
- Speculation
- Legitimate need

### *Debt Service*

The borrower must demonstrate a sufficient cash flow to cover debt service—the periodic mortgage payments. Typically, these are interest-only payments. Given the liquidity, cash flow, equity, and contingent liabilities associated with the credit of a typical developer, it may be difficult for the lender to make a determination about debt service.

### *Repayment of Principal at Maturity*

The borrower must demonstrate that it can repay principal at maturity. This can be evidenced by

- sufficient liquid resources to repay the loan in full at the end of the term (if the loan is nonrecourse—meaning the investor cannot force the lender to repurchase the loan);
- sufficient resources to construct a building on the parcel of land without financing; and
- access to an ADC loan.

Because the typical developer is unable to demonstrate the first two requirements listed above, the justification for the land acquisition loan is typically access to an ADC loan. To support a land acquisition loan on this basis, the developer must have a substantial track record.

### Development Experience

Developers must demonstrate clear and successful experience in

- acquiring parcels of land;
- processing plans through the local government authority where the property is located;
- constructing buildings;
- obtaining ADC loans; and
- leasing.

The size of the property acquired relative to a developer's other projects is an important consideration. For example, if a developer has experience in acquiring five acre parcels and constructing 60,000 square foot buildings, it might be difficult to support a loan where the developer is proposing to undertake the construction of a multiple building project on a 20 acre parcel of land.

### Land Planning Issues

A builder must obtain approval from local government authorities (typically planning commissions who report to a board of supervisors) prior to developing a parcel of land. It takes a considerable amount of time to obtain all local government approvals that allow for site development and construction. This exposes the lender to swings in local and national real estate markets (demand and supply) and the national economy (interest rates).

Lenders should consider all issues related to the development of the site, including the site development plan and building plan ("plans"), and the length of time required for a developer to obtain approval of the plans from local government authorities. At a minimum, the developer should provide architectural plans illustrating and outlining the specifications and design of the building to be constructed, and should reflect the applicable zoning and related building codes.

In the absence of plans, a developer may not have a complete understanding of the development timetable for a parcel of land. The time required for an architect and engineer to develop plans for submission to a local municipality can be considerable. The development and submission of plans to a local planning board and subsequent approval could take from 18 to 24 months.

### Zoning

There is the possibility that a parcel of land is not zoned for the use intended by the developer. For example, a parcel of land zoned residential must be rezoned to commercial prior to the construction of a building. To rezone a parcel of land, the developer must make application to a local government under specified procedures. There are three possible outcomes of the rezoning process:

1. The developer obtains the rezoning.
2. The rezoning is denied.
3. The rezoning is granted, however on onerous terms for the developer.

Should either (2) or (3) occur, the results could be disastrous to the lender, depending on the basis under which the land was purchased and financed.

If the land is purchased and financed based on its future value when rezoned, a denial or modification to an anticipated rezoning could severely impact value. As a result, a lender should base the loan and LTV ratio on the "as-is" value, not the "as-rezoned" value. Even in a situation where a property is successfully rezoned, rezoning land can take years, depending on the local municipality. As a result, a lender should insist that the builder develop a realistic timetable for rezoning land, developing plans, and obtaining an approval of plans.

### Request for Expedited Loan

While there could be many reasons why a developer requests a land acquisition loan, the loan may be needed immediately to acquire a parcel of land. For example, the developer may not have had sufficient time to apply for an ADC loan. A lender should be wary of this transaction, because the developer may not have had sufficient time to fully comprehend all requirements. The following concerns should be addressed:

- The myriad of zoning and municipal planning requirements to develop the land and construct a building
- Analysis of the physical characteristics of the land (soil and/or environmental)
- The parcel's future development potential or the type of structures that can be built on the land
- The supply and demand of competing space in the particular submarket
- The estimated costs to develop the land and construct the building, and sources for the ADC loan and ultimate permanent loan

### Speculation

A lender should be careful to understand the basis on which a developer is requesting a land acquisition loan. In contrast to a developer who acquires land for current projects or those in the near future, there is the possibility that a developer is seeking a loan to finance land speculation.

The developer may believe that a parcel of land can be purchased and "flipped," or sold at a profit to a third party. In the absence of a contract with a third party to acquire the land, this is probably the worst possible situation under which a lender could provide a land acquisition loan. The developer may be relying on unpredictable supply and demand conditions for raw land and the ability to locate a third party capable of purchasing the land.

### Legitimate Need

Many developers need interim, short-term loans to finance the acquisition of a piece of land while they are in the process of obtaining or closing an ADC loan. For example, a developer may have obtained a commitment for an ADC loan, which is in the process of closing. However, an interim loan is needed to facilitate the acquisition of the land prior to the expiration of a sales contract. This situation provides a bona fide opportunity for a careful lender, as opposed to the speculative situation previously described. It could also be that the same lender is in the process of closing the ADC loan and will provide the acquisition loan in anticipation of closing the construction financing.

# ■ Acquisition, Development, and Construction (ADC) Loan

An ADC loan finances the acquisition and development of land, and the construction of a building on that land. ADC loans involve many of the same risks as land acquisition loans and are similarly difficult to underwrite. Underwriting considerations include the following:

■ Debt service
■ Repayment of principal at maturity
■ Development experience
■ Land planning issues
■ Speculation versus preleasing
■ Refinancing shortfalls
■ Construction risk
■ Lease approval and tenant build-out
■ Loan servicing
■ Interest rate risk

## Debt Service

The developer must demonstrate sufficient cash flow to make the interest payments. It should be noted that it would be typical for a developer to request an *interest reserve*, which is a portion of the loan reserved for interest payments.

## Repayment of Principal at Maturity

Although a developer may sell a building and repay an ADC loan prior to its maturity, it is unlikely that the building reaches its potential value within this time frame. Either the developer is reluctant to sell the building and forgo the potential equity, or the value of the collateral on an "as is" basis is not sufficient to fully repay the loan. As a result, the ultimate repayment of an ADC loan is typically a mini-perm or permanent loan. Therefore, the developer must demonstrate the ability to develop the land and construct and lease the building by the expiration of the loan to create value to support a permanent loan.

## Development Experience

The developer must demonstrate a clear and solid track record in

■ acquiring parcels of land;
■ processing plans through the local government authority in which the property is located;
■ constructing buildings;
■ leasing; and
■ obtaining mini-perm or permanent loans.

The size of the property acquired relative to the developer's other projects is an important consideration, as well as the developer's property management experience.

### Land Planning Issues

Depending on the extent to which the developer has processed plans through the local municipality, land planning issues could be identical to those discussed under land acquisition loans.

However, it is generally standard for a parcel of land securing an ADC loan to be *ready-to-go*. This term means that the plans are approved and the developer has secured all required permits to allow for land development and construction, and there are no land planning or zoning issues remaining. Also, for a ready-to-go project, the borrower has

- anticipated and provided for bonding requirements (see *letters of credit* below);
- obtained bids; and
- secured contracts from the general contractor.

A lengthy time frame from acquisition of the land to actual development and construction exposes the lender to swings in local and national real estate markets (demand and supply) and the national economy (interest rates).

### Speculation Versus Preleasing

Because the value of the building has not yet been created, an ADC loan is predicated upon a future value, once the property has reached stabilized occupancy and operation. The appraisal obtained by a lender would make reference to this future value, which could be based on the following:

- The appraisal is completely supported by future leasing projections.
- Preleases obtained by the developer prior to closing the ADC loan support the appraisal.

Without preleasing, an ADC loan is speculative and relies on future projections for leasing. Because it could take anywhere from 18 to 24 months to complete a project, depending on the size and scope, it is difficult to predict future lease rates and terms.

For example, if an appraisal assumed that a 66,000 square foot building would be leased at $16 per square foot and market rents subsequently declined to $14 per square foot, the value of the building would be substantially affected. In this example, the $2 per square foot decline in rents would equate to a $132,000 reduction in the project's net operating income (NOI). Assuming a 10 percent capitalization (cap) rate, the value of the project would be reduced by $1,320,000 ($132,000 × 0.10).

The extent to which a developer can obtain preleases reduces the lender's reliance on future leasing projections. Continuing the example above, let's assume the developer has preleased 50 percent of the space, or 33,000 square feet. In this case, the $2 per square foot decline in market rents would result in a $66,000 reduction in NOI. Again, assuming a 10 percent cap rate, the project's value would decline by $660,000 ($66,000 × 0.10).

If a prelease was written prior to a decline in rents, the prospective tenant may desire to renegotiate the terms of the prelease. Also, the terms of preleases should be reviewed for early termination dates. If preleases terminate after one or two years, the leases would have to be renegotiated at market rates or the space leased to a new tenant.

Whether a project is based on future leasing or preleasing, the ADC lender is exposed to changes in future leasing markets. As a result, the building's future value should be supported by a stable and predictable leasing market. If new buildings are being constructed around the subject building, or if there are nearby ready-to-go parcels of land, a lender could be facing a serious supply and demand problem and a disastrous decline in market rents and value.

### Refinancing Shortfalls

The repayment of an ADC loan is likely a mini-perm or permanent loan. These loans are based on the future value of the project once completed. If an ADC loan is supported by a future value which is never realized, then a developer may be forced to inject additional equity into the project at the maturity of the ADC loan. This enables the developer to repay sufficient principal to support a permanent loan at the project's reduced value.

Assuming a mini-perm or permanent loan at 75 percent loan-to-value ratio (LTV), the $2 per square foot decline in market rents would require the developer to inject an additional $940,500 of equity:

|  | $16/SF | $14/SF |
|---|---|---|
| Rents | $1,056,000 | $ 924,000 |
| Vacancy (5%) | (52,800) | (46,200) |
| Net Revenues | 1,003,200 | 877,800 |
| Operating Expenses $6 SF | ( 396,000) | (396,000) |
| Net Operating Income | 607,200 | 481,800 |
| Value assuming a 10% cap rate | 6,072,000 | 4,818,000 |
| Loan at 75% LTV | 4,554,000 | 3,613,500 |

The difference between a 75% LTV loan at $16 per square foot and at $14 per square foot is the $940,500 of additional equity required.

### Construction Risk

A developer may only partially complete a project, forcing the lender to foreclose. Once a loan has defaulted, the lender must step into the developer's shoes and complete the project. Under these circumstances, it is likely that the relationships between the developer and contractors and consultants are strained, and the lender could be forced to resolve substantial conflicts prior to completing the project. As a result, the developer must demonstrate the ability to build the structure under consideration and have a significant track record in construction in the initial stages of the loan process. For example, a $10,000,000 ADC loan to a developer who has never constructed or managed a project would expose the lender to extreme construction risk.

Even developers with experience have had problems with general contractors. As a result, the financial wherewithal of the general contractor must also be assessed by the lender to determine the ability of the general contractor to perform under its contract. While the developer may have experience, a general contractor may not have the financial capacity to handle the project intended, or worse yet, the general contractor may not have a significant track record in constructing the type of building envisioned.

### Lease Approval and Tenant Build-Out

Once the shell of a building is completed, a developer will lease and complete the vacant space. This is where the real value is created.

Most lenders require borrowers to submit leases for approval. Leases contain many provisions, including the net rentable area, base rent, free rent allowances, the amount of operating expenses shared by the tenant, and the tenant improvement allowance. The terms of the leases should be compared by the lender to the original appraisal to ensure that value is being created consistent with earlier projections. Once the lease has been approved by the lender and executed by the tenant and borrower, the lender can fund tenant improvements (TI) as work is completed.

Prior to the lease being prepared, the developer undertakes a considerable amount of work, typically known as *space planning.* This is a significant effort, because individual tenants have different space requirements. While tenant build-out is closely related to construction, it is a unique process that requires a considerable amount of due diligence and expertise. If it is done improperly, a tenant may never occupy the space. A lender could have advanced considerable sums for TI without the anticipated creation of value.

### Loan Servicing

The servicing requirements related to a construction loan are considerable. The lender is expected to advance sums to the borrower as work is completed. To fund the borrower's requisition, the completed work must be inspected, title endorsements and lien waivers obtained, and the loan commitment must be reviewed to ensure that there are sufficient funds remaining to complete the project. This further reinforces the prerequisite that the developer have considerable experience, because a lender has to rely on the borrower to complete the project.

### Interest Rate Risk

Construction lenders face substantial interest rate risk, which can be difficult to determine since the time to acquire and develop land and construct a building can be considerable. Interest rate risk will be illustrated with respect to mini-perm loans.

## ■ Mini-Perm Loan

A mini-perm loan is an interim loan. It provides a developer with breathing room between the maturity of an ADC loan and the time a project has reached stabilized occupancy and is ready for permanent financing. Because the project is most likely completed and leased to a level sufficient to support debt service, the mini-perm loan does not involve debt service, repayment, land planning, and construction risk associated with land acquisition and ADC loans. However, the project must still be leased and ultimately refinanced with a permanent loan.

The mini-perm lender must consider a number of issues during underwriting:

- Debt service
- Repayment of principal at maturity
- Tenant improvements
- Existing leases
- Credit quality
- *As-is* value versus stabilized value
- Interest rate risk

### Debt Service

Because the project has probably not reached maximum occupancy, the project's net operating income (NOI) may not be sufficient to support principal and interest payments based on the amortization schedule or mortgage constant associated with a permanent loan. The NOI may, however, be sufficient to support interest-only payments.

### Repayment of Principal at Maturity

The repayment of the mini-perm loan is via a permanent loan. To support a permanent loan, the stabilized value of the project must be achieved and the NOI must be increased during the term of the mini-perm loan. As a result, the mini-perm lender must understand the terms of existing leases and assumptions for future leasing, and rely on the borrower to lease all vacant space and create the additional value and NOI consistent with the underwriting parameters of permanent lenders.

### Tenant Improvements

Because the developer may still have additional space to lease, the ability to cover the tenant improvement requirements resulting from future leasing must be demonstrated. Otherwise, the developer may not be able to finalize leases without funds to complete tenant space. For example, assuming that 20 percent of a 66,000 square foot building is vacant, and an average tenant improvement allowance is $10 per square foot, the developer would need to demonstrate $132,000 in available cash reserves to cover tenant improvements on the vacant space (66,000 × 0.20 × $10 per square foot). Depending on the level of NOI, future tenant improvements may be supported by existing cash flow.

### Existing Leases

The terms of existing leases must be clearly underwritten, because the borrower may have granted free rent allowances. As a result, the lender must be careful to understand the cash flow generated by existing leases. For example, a lease with 24 months free rent will not generate any income until the 25th month.

The maturity date of existing leases must also be understood, because the maturity date may be prior to the mini-perm loan. If the lease is above market, the borrower could lose the tenants upon lease expiration. Also, a permanent lender will not rely on leases with short terms and above market rents.

### Credit Quality

Should a property be filled with tenants who are not paying as agreed, it is unlikely that debt service can be covered. As a result, tenant payment records must be obtained along with financial statements of major tenants.

### As-Is *Value Versus Stabilized Value*

Although a project may be substantially leased and cash flows easy to determine, the lender is still exposed to uncertainty concerning future leasing. The extent of this risk depends on the amount of vacant space, the value of the property based on current leases in place and the expiration or termination dates of existing leases. Should tenants depart the premises at the expiration of existing leases, the leases have to be renegotiated at market rates or the space leased to new tenants.

While it is desirable to lend on the value of the property based on current leases, this may not be practical. The need for the mini-perm loan has probably arisen because of a matured ADC loan, which was based on a future value. Thus, lending based on the current lease approach would require the developer to inject a considerable amount of equity. Continuing with our example, the developer would have to inject an additional equity of $1,188,000 assuming an 80% occupancy level and an as-is value:

|  | Stabilized $16/SF | As Is $16/SF |
|---|---|---|
| Rents | $1,056,000 | $1,056,000 |
| Vacancy | ( 52,800) 5% | (211,200) 20% |
| Net Revenues | 1,003,200 | 844,800 |
| Operating Expenses $6/SF | (396,000) | ( 396,000) |
| Net Operating Income | 607,200 | 448,800 |
| Value assuming a 10% cap rate | 6,072,000 | 4,488,000 |
| Loan at 75% LTV | 4,554,000 | 3,366,000 |

In this case, the original ADC loan was based on 75% of the stabilized future value. However, the mini-perm loan was based on 75% of the value of the project *as-is*, i.e., 80% leased. Typically, the mini-perm loan is based on the stabilized future value so that a substantial equity contribution is not necessary. However, this reliance on future leasing could once again result in risk for the lender.

Continuing with our example, assuming that the remaining space (20%) is leased at $14 per square foot rather than $16, the extent of the leasing risk faced by the lender would be $188,100:

|  | 80% @ $16/SF | 20% @ $14/SF |
|---|---|---|
| Rents | $1,056,000 | $1,029,600 |
| Vacancy 5% | (52,800) | (51,480) |
| Net Revenues | 1,003,200 | 978,120 |
| Operating Expenses $6/SF | (396,000) | (396,000) |
| Net Operating Income | 607,200 | 582,120 |
| Value assuming a 10% cap rate | 6,072,000 | 5,821,200 |
| Loan at 75% LTV | 4,554,000 | 4,365,900 |

### Interest Rate Risk

Because most permanent lenders base loans on the debt coverage ratio (DCR = ratio of NOI to debt service), the mini-perm lender is exposed to interest rate risk.

In our example, the stabilized NOI of $607,200 (based on $16 per square foot) results in a DCR of 1.5×, assuming a loan amount of $4,554,000, with monthly payments of principal and interest based on a fixed-rate loan at 7.5% and a 25 year amortization. However, if interest rates rise to 8.0%, the lender is exposed to interest rate risk of $193,679, assuming a constant debt coverage requirement of 1.5×:

| Mortgage Rates | 7.5% | | 8.0% |
|---|---|---|---|
| Net Operating Income | $607,200 | | $607,200 |
| Principal & Interest | $403,844 | | $421,782 |
| Debt Coverage Ratio | 1.50× | | 1.44× |
| Loan at 1.5× DCR (8%) | | $4,360,321 | |
| Construction Loan | | 4,554,000 | |
| Deficit | | $(193,679) | |

## ■ Permanent Loan

A permanent loan is a long-term loan that allows a developer to finance a commercial project. The need for this loan usually arises because either an ADC loan or mini-perm loan has matured. Or, a permanent loan may have matured, and the lender holding the permanent loan may not have the ability or desire to extend the loan further. Additionally, a developer may want to refinance to obtain a lower interest rate.

At this point, the project has reached stabilized occupancy, value, and NOI. Because the property has achieved potential value (given existing market conditions), the property can be sold by the borrower to repay the loan at any point after the loan closes.

There are few remaining risks, but the lender must still be concerned with several issues:

- Debt service
- Repayment of principal at maturity
- Existing leases
- Credit risk
- Obsolescence

### Debt Service

Because the NOI has stabilized, it is probably sufficient to support principal and interest payments. The only issue now is whether or not the DCR and LTV are consistent with the credit policy standards of the lender. This is understood upfront when the loan is underwritten and closed. Subject to the credit quality of the tenants, the terms and conditions of existing leases and the stability of the leasing market, the DCR should be constant throughout the term of the loan.

### Repayment of Principal at Maturity

While the nature of a permanent loan is long-term, the lender should still consider future market conditions when estimating the future financing feasibility of the property. Because the loan is now amortizing, the loan balance at maturity should be compared with future leasing projections.

### Existing Leases

Because a project has most likely reached stabilized occupancy (i.e., 95 percent), the permanent lender can rely on current leases to cover debt service and an *as-is* or completed and stabilized value. However, the permanent lender is exposed to the same risk as a mini-perm lender with regard to the expiration of existing leases. Leases that expire have to be renegotiated at existing market conditions or the space leased to a new tenant.

Leasing risk for a permanent lender is tied to the stability of the leasing market and the difference between rents on existing leases and current market conditions. For example, a lease to a tenant occupying 33,000 square feet, or 50 percent of a 66,000 square foot building, at $16 per square foot, maturing in one year, would have to be renegotiated at market conditions at maturity. If current market rates are $14 per square foot, there could be a significant reduction in the cash flow of the project, and thus its value.

### Credit Risk

A permanent lender is also exposed to credit risk with regard to major or significant tenants. For example, if a tenant who occupies 50 percent of a 66,000 square foot building experiences cash flow problems or, worse yet, files for bankruptcy protection, lease payments may become delinquent. Such a delinquency could lead to default of the loan if the developer is unwilling or unable to cover the shortfall. In addition, it may be difficult to evict the tenant, because the tenant may have legal rights to continue occupancy during a default in the lease. In this case, the space cannot be leased to a new tenant.

To underwrite credit risk, the permanent lender should obtain financial statements and payment histories on major tenants. Also, any new tenants should be carefully scrutinized, because their leases are not seasoned.

### Obsolescence

Another risk faced by the permanent lender is the age and type of building being financed. An older building may need a considerable amount of deferred mainte-nance (i.e., a new roof) or may contain asbestos. Also, the building may not be competitive with newer buildings.

## ■ Letters of Credit

Municipalities in which projects are located typically require developers to sign development agreements with regard to the installation of on-site and off-site improvements. The municipalities require developers to secure the development agreements with bonds from bonding companies or letters of credit from financial institutions.

The amount and term of letters of credit can vary considerably between jurisdictions. Letters of credit can be *called* or *drawn* by a beneficiary (local governments) upon a default under the agreement by the developer. Most often, ADC lenders issue letters of credit.

Consider an example where $2,000,000 of the total project cost is related to off-site and on-site improvements. A local government may require the developer to post a letter of credit equal to 120 percent of the improvements, in this case $2,400,000. The letter of credit would favor the local government body, issued on the account of the developer and payable to the municipality, should the developer default under the development agreement. In addition, the letter of credit could contain *ever-green* language and be automatically renewable for an indefinite period of time.

Because the typical ADC loan commitment provides financing for the infrastructure covered by the development agreement, and the construction lender monitors a project closely during construction, a lender may not believe that a letter of credit involves significant risk. However, should a municipality call a letter of credit due to default under a development agreement, the local government could present the lender with a site draft for the entire letter of credit, regardless of the extent to which a project is complete. In the above example, while the developer may have completed $2,000,000 in improvements (and the lender funded the improvements), the county could still present the lender with a site draft for $2,400,000.

The ability of a local government to undertake such an action depends on the terms of the development agreement and letter of credit. However, most letters of credit provide the beneficiary with the right to present the lender with a site draft for the entire amount of the letter of credit at the default of the developer.

## ■ Forward Commitment

A forward commitment is a promise to provide permanent financing in the future, once a project has reached stabilized occupancy. Most ADC lenders require the developer to obtain a forward commitment, so that the ADC lender has some assurance that the ADC loan will be repaid at maturity.

Lenders who provide a forward commitment essentially reserve a block of funds for a specific borrower and project and fund the permanent loan in the future when certain underwriting considerations are addressed. These include the following:

- Loan-to-value (LTV) ratio
- Appraisal
- Debt coverage ratio
- Occupancy level

As a result, forward commitments are nothing more than an indication that a lender may make a loan in the future on certain conditions. Moreover, the forward commitment may not provide the developer with an interest rate cap. Given the conditional nature of a forward commitment, an ADC lender should not rely on it totally as a source for repayment.

## ■ Summary

The type of commercial loan or financing needed by a developer is directly tied to the stage of project completion and to the developer's specific requirements. Opportunities to finance a project are less risky as the project is completed.

As a project is completed, future underwriting considerations, such as leasing and interest rates, are easier to quantify and predict. Since each type of loan exposes the lender to certain general underwriting risks, any loan request from a developer must be well-supported and understood by the lender prior to processing and underwriting.

## ■ Chapter 4 Review Questions

1. Match the description with the appropriate term.

   **a.** Mini-perm loan

   **b.** Permanent loan

   **c.** Land acquisition loan

   **d.** Acquisition, Development, and Construction loan (ADC)

   _____ A long-term loan that provides permanent financing

   _____ A loan made for the purpose of purchasing land only, not improvements on or to the land

   _____ A loan made to finance the acquisition and development of raw land and the construction of a building on that land

   _____ An interim commercial real estate loan made in conjunction with a construction loan and usually three to five years in duration

2. Which of the following is NOT one of the three ways developers can demonstrate that they can repay principal at maturity under a land acquisition loan?

   **a.** Access to an ADC loan

   **b.** Access to a permanent loan

   **c.** Sufficient liquid resources to repay the loan at the end of the term

   **d.** Sufficient resources to construct a building on the parcel of land without financing

3. Check four underwriting considerations that apply to BOTH land acquisition and ADC loans.

   _____ Debt service

   _____ Land planning

   _____ Construction risk

   _____ Tenant buy-out

   _____ Developer experience

   _____ Repayment of principal at maturity

4. In order to support a land acquisition loan, a developer must have a substantial

   **a.** debt service.

   **b.** track record.

   **c.** property portfolio.

   **d.** development team.

5. All of the following are typical underwriting considerations for a forward commitment EXCEPT

   **a.** appraisal.

   **b.** occupancy level.

   **c.** debt coverage ratio.

   **d.** interest rate cap.

   **e.** loan-to-value (LTV).

6. ADC lenders most often issue letters of credit.

   **a.** True

   **b.** False

# Commercial Loan Documentation

## learning objectives

*Upon completion of this chapter, you should be able to*

- identify common commercial real estate loan documents;

- recognize important aspects of a guaranty;

- name key elements of a promissory note;

- name key elements of a mortgage; and

- distinguish two principal legal theories regarding the nature of a lender's interest under the mortgage.

## ■ Introduction

This Chapter presents a summary of the loan documents most commonly used by commercial real estate lenders. The first part of this Chapter lists and briefly summarizes key documents that are produced by a lender or legal counsel in connection with commercial real estate lending. The second and third parts address key elements of the promissory note and the mortgage or deed of trust. These items constitute the most critical and complex of the commercial real estate loan documents.

## ■ Commercial Loan Documentation

Commercial loans secured by non-real estate collateral are usually governed by a loan agreement. The loan agreement sets forth a number of representations, warranties, and covenants binding the parties, in addition to repayment terms and interest provisions.

A loan agreement is generally not used in a commercial mortgage lending transaction. The representations and covenants are drafted into the mortgage as required by the lender to address the risks presented by a particular borrower or transaction. Provisions regarding the lender's remedies upon the borrower's default under the note are incorporated by cross-reference to the mortgage. An array of separate agreements and contracts executed together with the note and mortgage may impose further obligations to be performed by the borrower and provide additional remedies to the lender. The loan documents most commonly used by commercial lenders are presented below.

### Loan Commitment

The loan commitment letter confirms the lender's offer to make the loan and summarizes the essential terms of the transaction. Typically, the commitment letter sets forth the following:

- Amount of the loan
- Interest rate
- Maturity date
- Repayment terms
- Prepayment options
- Collateral securing the obligation
- Identity of any proposed guarantors
- Any preconditions to closing that must be satisfied by the borrower

In addition, the commitment letter sets forth the principal documents to be executed by the borrower and a summary of their terms. To protect the lender, the commitment letter terminates on a specific date, by which time the borrower must execute the commitment and provide that the commitment will be canceled

- if a material adverse change in the borrower's business occurs, or
- if the borrower fails to comply with the terms of the commitment.

### Promissory Note

The promissory note evidences the borrower's obligation to the lender and is discussed in further detail later in this lesson. It sets forth the essential terms of the borrower's obligation, such as

- principal amount of the obligation;
- interest rate; and
- maturity date.

Additional provisions address prepayment, security, and other matters.

### Mortgage or Deed of Trust

The mortgage is the document that provides the lender with a security interest in the borrower's real property as collateral for the debt. Unlike the customary practice in commercial lending, in which a separate loan agreement governs the transaction, the mortgage may set forth significant terms of the transaction with regard to the

- borrower's representations and warranties;
- borrower's debt; and
- environmental matters.

## *Guaranty*

The guaranty substantiates a promise by a third party, often an affiliate or principal of the borrower, obligating the third party to pay the obligation of the borrower in the event of default under the obligation to the lender.

The guarantor may provide additional collateral as security for the guarantor's obligations. The critical issues in the drafting and preparation of the guaranty are as follows:

1. Identification of the receipt of adequate consideration on the part of the guarantor from the borrower in exchange for the delivery of the guaranty

2. A clear statement that the lender has the right to proceed against the guarantor under the guaranty without first pursuing or exhausting any remedies against the borrower

3. A waiver of subrogation by the guarantor

The guaranty should clearly acknowledge that the guarantor has received an economic benefit by virtue of its delivery of the guaranty. This avoids the later assertion of a defense to the enforcement of the guaranty based on lack of consideration. If the guarantor is a parent corporation or a principal of the borrower, the value provided by the continued economic viability of the borrower is adequate consideration.

A more difficult issue is presented in the situation where a subsidiary is guarantying the debt of a corporate parent. Courts have held that when a subsidiary guarantees the debt of a parent shareholder, such guaranty may be avoided under fraudulent conveyance laws if it is demonstrated that the subsidiary/guarantor did not receive reasonably equivalent value for the guaranty and was rendered insolvent by the delivery of the guaranty. The lending community has responded to these court decisions through the use of the net worth guaranty, under which the subsidiary/guarantor's liability is limited to a percentage of its net worth, thus rendering it impossible for the guarantor to be rendered insolvent by the guaranty.

The use of the net worth guaranty has been criticized, however, because the definition of the guarantor's net worth is subject to dispute. Reasonable individuals could legitimately justify substantially varied valuations of the guarantor's net worth, resulting in commercial uncertainty and raising a litigable issue.

As an alternative, some bankruptcy courts, which have considered a guarantor's liability under the fraudulent conveyance provisions of the Bankruptcy Code, have suggested that it is not appropriate to value a guaranty at the total face amount of the debt guaranteed; rather, the total of the guarantor's liability is discounted by the probability of recovery against the guaranty. Accordingly, the incremental value of a net worth guaranty versus a full guaranty may depend on the state of the law in a given jurisdiction.

At a minimum, the guaranty should anticipate any fraudulent conveyance defenses by the guarantor by providing a representation that the guarantor is not rendered insolvent by the making of the guaranty. The drafter, weighing the potential risks versus the benefits, should carefully consider the use of the net worth guaranty.

Until the enactment of the Bankruptcy Reform Act of 1994, the decision of the Seventh Circuit in *Levit v. Ingersoll Rand Financial Corp., et al. (In re Deprizio)*, 874 F.2d 1186 (7th Cir. 1989) was adopted as binding precedent in a number of jurisdictions. The case was brought by the trustee of a bankrupt construction company seeking to recover from a lender the fraudulent transfer payments made on debt guaranteed by insiders of the company in the year prior to the bankruptcy. Under traditional bankruptcy practice, a lender is only liable for payments in the 90 days prior to the filing. The extended one year preference recovery period is applied under certain circumstances when the payment is made for the benefit of an insider of the debtor.

The court in *Deprizio* decided in favor of the trustee of the bankrupt company, holding the lender liable to disgorge payments made during the year prior to the borrower's bankruptcy filing. Under the *Deprizio* analysis, payments made by a borrower during the year prior to the filing of the bankruptcy petition that have the effect of reducing an insider guarantor's contingent liability on its guaranty may be recovered from the lender, even though the lender is not an insider. In the court's view, the payments, although made to an outside creditor, benefited the insiders by reducing their financial exposure on their guaranties.

As with the *upstream guaranty* problem, the lending community responded to the *Deprizio* holding with a drafting solution, by introducing into the guaranty a waiver of subrogation. Under the subrogation waiver, the guarantor waives its rights to recover from the borrower sums paid to the lender pursuant to the guaranty, and thus the guarantor is not a creditor under the *Deprizio* analysis. The payment made by the borrower to the lender during the preference period is not made "to or for the benefit of a creditor" (under the Bankruptcy Code analysis) because the guarantor has no rights as a creditor of the borrower.

The *Deprizio* doctrine was widely criticized for widening the scope of the bankruptcy trustee's recovery powers beyond the range intended by Congress. The Bankruptcy Reform Act of 1994 overruled the *Deprizio* line of cases by specifically providing that a trustee cannot recover a preferential transfer from a transferee that is not an insider. With this express limitation on the trustee's power in place, it can reasonably be expected that the *Deprizio* doctrine will no longer be relevant to commercial lending transactions.

It is important, from the lender's perspective, that the guaranty provides that the lender is not obligated to exhaust remedies against the borrower prior to seeking recovery from the guarantor. This provision maximizes the lender's options in the event of default under the loan documents, although it is generally a heavily negotiated point. Typically, the guarantor attempts to negotiate a requirement that the lender exhaust all remedies against the borrower prior to seeking recovery from the guarantor, particularly in the case of an unsecured personal guaranty.

The guaranty commonly includes a number of clauses to derive the full benefit of the guarantor's commitment. In order to maximize the value of the guaranty, the guaranty generally provides that the guarantor's obligation remains in force until all of the obligations of the borrower are repaid. The guarantor in the guaranty also expressly waives consent to changes in the nature of the underlying obligation, such as increases in the amount of the loan, release or exchange of collateral, or changes in term of the loan.

In the case of a guaranty from married individuals, the effect of Federal Reserve Regulation B and the restrictions it places on requiring a spouse's signature on an obligation primarily of the other spouse must be observed. If a guaranty is unsecured, it is generally preferable to include both spouses as guarantors so that the obligation can be enforced against their joint property. Under Regulation B, a creditor may not require the signature of an obligor's spouse on a credit instrument (such as a guaranty) if the obligor alone qualifies under the lender's standards of creditworthiness for the obligation. However, Regulation B provides an exception to the restrictions. It makes it permissible to require a spouse's signature on a debt instrument when necessary under state law to obtain that signature in order to make available to the lender, upon default, the additional property necessary to satisfy the lender's objective credit standards.

In addition to guarantying the borrower's obligation to the lender, the guaranty should include, as part of the guarantor's obligations payable under the guaranty, the costs of enforcement of the guaranty. The guaranty should also set forth standard provisions to expedite the enforcement of the lender's rights, such as waiver of demand and waiver of jury trial, to the extent enforceable under local law.

## Assignment of Leases and Rents

While a mortgage typically includes leases and rents as a component of the collateral granted, a lender may have the borrower execute a separate assignment of leases and rents. The separate document will more fully state the

- borrower's obligations, and
- lender's rights in the event of an occurrence of default under the loan documents.

Until recently, lenders typically used a collateral assignment for the assignment of leases and rents. Under the collateral assignment, the lender's right to income from the property under the assignment of rents was contingent upon the occurrence of default by the borrower. A line of court decisions, however, cast into doubt the utility of the collateral assignment in the context of a bankruptcy by the borrower. Under the Bankruptcy Code, the general rule is that a pre-petition security interest does not reach post-petition property in bankruptcy. The Bankruptcy Code provides exceptions in certain circumstances, including loans on *rents and profits* of collateral to the extent provided in the applicable agreement and state law (subject to modification based on the equities of the case). A number of bankruptcy courts held that the lender's rights under the assignment are not perfected under state law until the lender takes *additional steps* to realize its security interest in the rents. These additional steps may be relatively minimal, such as delivery of notice to direct rents to the lender, or be as drastic as a motion for appointment of a receiver. Under this line of cases, the failure of the lender to take action prior to the filing of a bankruptcy petition by the borrower may result in the rents collected after the filing of the petition being paid into the bankruptcy estate.

As a consequence of these decisions, the preferred form of assignment of leases and rents became an absolute assignment. Under the terms of an absolute assignment, the borrower makes an immediately effective assignment of rents to the lender and the lender grants to the borrower a license to receive the rents, revocable upon the occurrence of an event of default. The lender, as a result of this structure, is contractually entitled to receive the rents from the beginning of the life of the loan and the issue as to whether the lender's rights need to be perfected does not arise. The Bankruptcy Reform Act of 1994 resolved this controversy by adding a separate section for rents that deleted the reference to state law. Thus, post-petition rents constitute collateral of a pre-petition assignment of rents, notwithstanding the failure to obtain a receiver or otherwise to exercise an assignment of rents prior to bankruptcy, as may be required to assert interests under state law.

### Security Agreement

In addition to requiring the borrower to execute the documents conveying a security interest in the real property and the rights thereunder, the lender may also have the borrower execute a security agreement providing the lender with a security interest in personal property used in connection with the real property under Article 9 of the Uniform Commercial Code. As with the assignment of leases and rents, abbreviated language creating the security interest is typically provided in the mortgage.

If appropriate, the lender may choose to have the additional benefit of the collateral granted under a full security agreement. In order to perfect the lender's interest in the additional collateral, the borrower must execute financing statements and they must be filed in all the appropriate public records. The mortgage provides a covenant by the borrower to cooperate in the filing of the financing statements and all documents necessary to perfect the lender's security interest.

### Assignment of Management Agreement

In those situations where the borrower employs an agent to manage the property, the lender may require the borrower to assign its rights to receive the services of the management agent to the lender. The assignment typically provides for the agent's consent to the assignment. The assignment permits the lender to avail itself of the services of the existing management company, which is familiar with the property and maintains records with regard to its operation.

In circumstances where the borrower and management agent are affiliated, the management agent may be required to

- subordinate its rights in the management fees to the lender, and
- agree to withdraw as management agent on lender demand in the event the lender succeeds to the borrower's interest after a default under the loan.

### Replacement Reserve Agreement

This agreement requires the borrower to deposit various sums with the lender to create a replacement reserve account. The purpose of the replacement reserve is to provide a fund from which the borrower can draw to pay for anticipated replacements of major items on the property such as appliances, heating and air conditioning equipment, roof, and similar capital improvements. In addition, this agreement typically provides for an assignment of the replacement reserve to the lender as additional security for all the borrower's obligations to the lender.

### Completion/Repair Agreement

This is another document typically executed in connection with multifamily loans and requires the borrower to perform various repairs and improvements to the property within a specified period of time. The agreement allows the lender to review and approve the repairs made to the mortgaged property. The borrower's failure to comply with the terms of the completion/repair agreement is considered default under the general obligations to the lender, entitling the lender to foreclose against the property. As with the replacement reserve agreement, it may also require that a fund be established and held as additional security by the lender and drawn on by the borrower as the repairs are completed.

### Certificate of Borrower

This document is often executed in connection with non-real estate commercial loans. It is essentially an estoppel certificate, in which the borrower makes various representations relating to the mortgaged property and the borrower's financial status, and reaffirms the representations and warranties made in the loan documents.

### Agreement to Amend, Comply, or Correct

This agreement obligates the borrower to cooperate with any necessary remedial action with regard to the loan documents. While it does not obligate the borrower to undertake substantive amendments required by the lender, it requires the borrower to comply with the lender's request to correct errors in the documentation of the transaction.

### Operations and Maintenance Agreement

The Operations and Maintenance Agreement is executed in connection with a loan secured by multifamily property when some environmental concern, such as the presence of minimal asbestos, will persist after the loan is closed. Under the agreement, the borrower is obligated to develop and comply with an operations and maintenance (O&M) program to monitor and control the environmental condition on the property securing the loan. Failure to comply with the O&M program is considered a default under the loan and entitles the lender to all the remedies provided under the loan documents.

### Title Insurance Policy

The lender requires a policy of title insurance insuring the lien of its mortgage. In addition, the lender may require additional endorsements to the policy providing additional coverages as necessitated by the nature of the transaction. Endorsements that are customarily requested by the lender include, when appropriate, the variable-rate mortgage endorsement (which insures the lender against unenforceability or loss of priority of the lien by reason of changes in the rate of interest provided in the loan documents) and the affirmative coverage endorsement (which insures the lender against loss caused by covenants, conditions, restrictions, or encroachments on the property that can impair the lien of the mortgage). Other less frequently used endorsements insure against more obscure risks, and additional coverages required by specific transactions may be negotiated with the title insurance company as necessary.

# ■ **Note**

The note evidences the borrower's obligation to the lender and is essentially a written promise by the borrower to repay the lender in accordance with the terms of the note. The law governing the note in the commercial mortgage loan transaction is the Uniform Commercial Code (UCC), in spite of the fact that the UCC does not generally cover real estate transactions.

This section discusses in general terms the formalities of the note as they relate to the commercial mortgage loan transaction. We refer the reader to the UCC and related authorities for a more specific discussion of the issues presented in this section.

## *Capacity*

As a preliminary matter, the borrower must have the capacity to enter into the obligation so that the obligation is enforceable. In the case of an individual, this is defined as a person of sound mind over the age of 18 years. In most cases, however, in the context of a commercial mortgage loan, the borrower is a corporation or a partnership.

It is the duty of lender's counsel to undertake at least minimal due diligence by way of a review of the borrower's constituent documents and a request for certificate of good standing or qualification to do business in the relevant jurisdiction. In addition, lender's counsel should obtain an opinion of the borrower's counsel as to matters relating to the maker's power and authority to enter into the transaction. Where the borrower is a trust or unincorporated association, special problems regarding status, authorization, and enforceability may exist and must be addressed.

## *Multiple Borrowers and Joint and Several Liability*

Where there are multiple borrowers in the loan transaction, each of the borrowers should appear as a maker on the note. Under the legal doctrine of joint and several liability, each of the multiple borrowers is liable for the entire amount of the indebtedness to the lender. The note should prominently state that all makers are jointly and severally liable for the entire amount of the indebtedness evidenced by the note.

## *Transferability and Negotiability*

As a general principle, all essential terms of the obligation are intended to be ascertainable from the face of the note, which sets forth the

■ total principal amount of the indebtedness, and
■ borrower's explicit promise to pay all amounts due under the note to the lender.

Article 3 of the Uniform Commercial Code requires specific language in order for the note to be negotiable and the transferee of the note to maintain status as a holder in due course. Under the UCC, the transferee's status as a holder in due course permits the holder to take the note free of any defenses, which may be asserted against the original payee. While the legal formalities of negotiation and holder in due course status are complex, the UCC requires, at a minimum, the use of the words *to the order of* in order for the note to be endorsed to subsequent payee to preserve the payee's status as a holder in due course. This ability to transfer and negotiate the obligation is essential for a lender seeking to sell the note in the secondary mortgage market or assign the note to a third party. In addition, the ability to transfer the note permits the lender to maintain a full range of options if the note goes into default, such as selling the obligation at a discount to another lender or transferring the debt for disposition by an asset manager.

### Maturity

The maturity date is the date on which all outstanding principal and accrued interest owed to the lender by the borrower is payable.

Alternatively, the note may be structured as a demand note whereby the entire principal and interest accrued may be payable to the lender upon the lender's demand. As with the term note, however, a demand note states a final maturity date on which the entire amount of principal and interest is due. A demand note is typically used in a revolving loan under the terms of which the borrower can obtain advances up to a maximum principal amount.

### Interest

The interest rate to be charged by the lender on the outstanding principal balance of the loan is set forth prominently in the text of the note. The note also describes in detail the method by which interest is calculated. The interest rate may be a fixed-rate, a predetermined rate that stays constant through the term of the loan, or a *floating* or adjustable-rate, which adjusts from time to time during the term of the loan. The floating rate adjusts in accordance with fluctuations in an index, such as the average yield on treasury bills during a stated period, the prime rate or, increasingly, an index known as LIBOR (the London Inter Bank Offered Rate). Additional interest in excess of the index rate, the margin, is added to the index rate to determine the total interest to be charged on the outstanding balance due under the note. The note will also provide for additional interest to be charged in the event of default under the note.

### Prepayment

The note typically addresses whether, and under what conditions, the borrower may prepay all or a portion of principal. Many methods are used to assess prepayment charges. They are typically designed to preserve the lender's anticipated profit on the loan to the greatest degree possible.

Prepayment provisions may be optional, under which all or a portion of the obligation may be prepaid at the borrower's election, or mandatory, under which the borrower may be required to prepay the loan upon the occurrence of a certain event. Various jurisdictions have statutes prohibiting or restricting the application of prepayment charges or penalties.

The assessment of interest and prepayment penalties may also be subject to statutory usury prohibitions. State usury laws place a restriction on the total amount of interest that may be assessed on the principal amount of the loan. A violation of usury law may have drastic consequences for the lender; in some jurisdictions the lender may forfeit the right to receive any interest on the loan. As a drafting solution to the harsh consequences of the application of usury statutes, the note will provide that in the event that a portion of interest charged is deemed to be usurious, the note shall bear interest only at the maximum rate allowed by law.

### Events of Default and Remedies

A number of events of default may be enumerated in the note. The obvious event of default is the borrower's failure to pay the lender in accordance with the terms of the note. The note may also be cross-defaulted so that the failure by the borrower to perform other obligations to the lender constitutes default under the note. In the context of the commercial mortgage loan, an event of default under the mortgage securing the obligation is deemed an event of default under the note. The major remedy for default under the note is immediate acceleration of the entire outstanding principal due under the note.

The note also contains a number of provisions which aid the lender in promptly enforcing its rights against the borrower, including:

- a waiver of demand;
- notice of dishonor; and
- presentment and protest.

These waivers enable the lender to immediately exercise its remedies without engaging in the technical legal formalities required by the common law prior to enforcing its rights. Depending on the jurisdiction, the note may provide for waivers of objections to prejudgment remedies and trial by jury. In jurisdictions where they are recognized, these provisions permit the lender to attach or garnish the assets of the borrower prior to obtaining a judgment on the note.

Other jurisdictions also enforce cognovit or confession of judgment clauses whereby the maker empowers the lender or its attorney to enter judgment by confession against the maker in court. The availability of objections to waivers or prejudgment attachments or confessions of judgment, however, varies from state to state and their validity is often the subject of litigation on due process grounds.

## ■ Mortgage

The mortgage is the document that provides the lender with a security interest in the borrower's real property. As noted previously, the terms of a non-real estate commercial loan are usually governed by a loan agreement, setting forth

- representations and warranties of the borrower;
- negative covenants and financial reporting covenants; and
- interest and repayment terms.

By contrast, the terms of the typical commercial mortgage loan are drafted into the note and mortgage, and representations supplementing the standard covenants regarding the mortgaged property required by the lender are incorporated into the mortgage.

There are two principal legal theories with regard to the nature of the lender's interest under the mortgage—the title and lien theories. Under the title theory, the mortgage is a conveyance of a fee interest to the mortgagee, subject to defeasance (reconveyance back to the mortgagor) on the payment or satisfaction of the loan by the borrower. The alternative theory of the mortgage, the lien theory, holds that the lender does not have title under the mortgage but only a security interest.

The practical significance of the distinction is that under the title theory of mortgage, the mortgagee's title gives lenders the right to immediate possession of the mortgaged property at the occurrence of an event of default under the loan. The right of possession carries with it the right to protect against waste (deterioration of the property) and collect rents and profits.

Another form of mortgage often used is the deed of trust. Under the deed of trust, the real property is conveyed to a third party in trust to hold as security for the payment of the obligation to the lender. On the occurrence of an event of default under the obligation secured by the deed of trust, the lender has the power to compel the trustee to sell the property in satisfaction of the obligation. This lesson focuses on the mortgage form of real estate encumbrance under the title theory of mortgage, but the concepts are fundamentally the same when a deed of trust is used to secure the obligation.

## Formal Legal Requirements

The mortgage has a number of formal legal requirements. These requirements may vary according to state law, and generally include a(n)

- granting clause;
- description of the real property collateral;
- description of the obligation being secured; and
- agreement to pay the underlying indebtedness.

The granting clause of the mortgage contains a recitation of consideration followed by the words *grants and conveys* or similar language, and a reference to certain real property that is described by a formal legal description of the property according to its metes and bounds. In addition, the granting clause includes various appurtenant rights to the interest in the real property. These appurtenant rights include all

- rights associated with the fee interest, including easements and riparian rights;
- buildings and fixtures located on the property;
- rights to rents, issues, and profits;
- rights to insurance proceeds; and
- proceeds received by the borrower in connection with the collateral granted under the mortgage.

The granting clause is typically followed by a habendum clause that defines the extent of the lender's interest in the property; the estate granted to the lender is deemed void upon payment in full of the obligations secured by the mortgage.

The mortgage outlines the

- principal terms of the obligation being secured;
- principal amount of the indebtedness; and
- maturity date.

### Representations, Warranties, and Covenants

The commercial real estate mortgage contains a number of representations and warranties by the borrower with regard to the property and the borrower's status in relation to the property. The customary provisions include a representation that:

1. the borrower has title to the property subject to certain permitted encumbrances;
2. the delivery of the mortgage does not conflict with any existing agreements or laws to which the borrower is subject; and
3. no additional consents of third parties are required for the delivery of the mortgage.

### Environmental Representations and Indemnification

Among the most important representations made by the borrower under the mortgage are representations regarding the environmental status of the property. This is a direct result of the proliferation of state and federal environmental legislation that imposes strict liability on property owners.

The environmental clause in a mortgage, at a minimum, prohibits the borrower from storing any hazardous materials on the premises or permitting any discharge of such materials. More stringent requirements may be imposed by the lender, however. These requirements may include

- detailed representations regarding the present condition of the property, and
- affirmative obligations from the borrower to notify the lender of any adverse occurrences regarding environmental conditions on the property or notices from regulatory authorities.

The mortgage may also provide the lender with the right to enter the property to evaluate environmental conditions. This may permit the lender to

- make intrusive inspections;
- engage consultants; and
- take remedial action at the expense of the borrower (as necessary).

Also, a lender may require the borrower to hold the lender harmless for any losses incurred which stem from environmental claims. Given the broad impact of environmental legislation and aggressive enforcement of these laws at all levels of government, it is extremely critical to the lender that all possible environmental contingencies are addressed in full.

### Preservation of the Collateral

In the mortgage, the borrower also makes a number of ongoing covenants with regard to its maintenance of the property. At a minimum, these obligations require the borrower to

- keep the property in good order; and
- protect the priority of the lender's lien from the assertion of liens for governmental charges that may become due prior to the lender's mortgage.

The terms of the mortgage require that the borrower pay all assessments relating to the property, including such items as taxes, sewer use fees, and water charges, for which the assessing authority may be entitled to a lien.

The lender may require the borrower, at the lender's request, to deposit into escrow with the lender an amount sufficient to pay all government charges. Such escrow amounts are paid together with principal and interest payments in a manner that permits the total amount of such escrow payments to accrue in full when due. This provides the lender with additional security by requiring the borrower to make provision for charges which could become a competing lien against the property which the lender might have to pay in the event of a foreclosure.

The obligation on the part of the borrower to maintain the property in good order includes an obligation not to commit waste and to promptly repair any damage or dangerous condition on the property. The terms of the mortgage prohibit the borrower from removing anything of value from the mortgaged property or from making substantial alterations without the lender's consent. The lender is generally entitled under the terms of the mortgage to inspect the mortgaged property upon reasonable notice to the borrower to ensure compliance with the mortgagee's maintenance provisions.

The borrower is required to maintain hazard insurance insuring the improvements on the property from casualty loss. The insurance clause also provides that in the event of the borrower's failure to maintain insurance, the lender has the right to obtain insurance on the property and add the premiums paid to principal due under the loan. The obligation to maintain insurance also requires that the lender be named as loss payee in the case of any payment on the policy. In the event of a payment under the policy and at the option of the lender, the proceeds may be applied to the indebtedness secured by the mortgage or to the costs of the repair of the damage to the property.

The application of insurance proceeds is a frequently negotiated point in commercial mortgage loan transactions. The borrower or legal counsel will seek the right to retain the insurance proceeds in the absence of an event of default.

### *Leasing the Mortgaged Property*

The mortgage typically

- restricts the borrower's right to lease the property in whole or in part; and
- requires the written consent of the lender to any leases entered into by the borrower.

To the extent that the borrower maintains leases with tenants on the property, terms of the mortgage require that the lender comply with its obligations under the leases affecting the property. The lender is granted the right to examine such leases and to subordinate the lien of the mortgage to any leases in force from time to time with regard to the mortgaged property.

The mortgage also grants the lender a security interest in any security deposits maintained by the borrower in connection with leases affecting the mortgaged property. In addition, the lender may require that all leases affecting the mortgaged property contain provisions specifically providing that the leases entered into are subordinate to the mortgage and that the tenant is required to attorn to the lender upon the lender's acquisition of the title to the property. The lender, however, may accept or reject such attornment at its discretion. The borrower may attempt to modify the restrictions on leasing by negotiating a provision providing that only leases in excess of a certain term, such as two to three years, require the lender's consent.

## Books and Records

In addition to the lender's right to physically inspect the property, the lender is provided with the right to inspect books and records maintained by the borrower in connection with its use and operation of the property. The borrower may be required to deliver financial statements to the lender with regard to the operation of the property, such as rent rolls, and the overall financial condition of the borrower, including balance sheets and income and loss statements.

## Condemnation

The mortgage also addresses the parties' rights upon condemnation of the mortgaged property. The condemnation provision of the mortgage typically provides that the borrower notify the lender of any action or proceeding relating to condemnation or other governmental taking. The borrower is authorized to appear in court and defend any such action or proceeding, or the lender may be appointed as attorney-in-fact for the borrower to appear in proceedings relating to condemnation of the property. Proceeds of any condemnation must be paid directly to the lender, unless the right to receive such proceeds is waived by the lender. The condemnation proceeds are to be applied to the outstanding amounts due under the loan and the balance paid to the mortgagee.

## Modification

The drafter of the mortgage generally anticipates that the loan securing the mortgage or the mortgage itself may be modified at some time in the future. Accordingly, the mortgage provides that any agreements relating to the extension of the indebtedness secured by the loan or modifications of the terms of the underlying debt will not affect the priority of the mortgage nor limit the rights of the lender with regard to the mortgaged property. This provision also provides that any waiver of rights of the lender under the loan documents will not affect the lender's right to exercise its remedies upon a later default.

## Estoppel Certificates

The mortgage also provides that the borrower shall, within a specified period of time, furnish the lender with an estoppel certificate. An estoppel certificate is a written statement setting forth the sum secured by the mortgage and stating that no rights of setoff, counterclaim, or other defenses exist against the obligation secured by the mortgage.

## Default and Remedies

For purposes of enforcement of the mortgage, the critical provisions of the mortgage are the provisions relating to the borrower's default. While the obvious events of default are failure to make payments on the obligation secured by the mortgage, the mortgage may also recite a number of other events of default.

Common events of default include

- filing by the borrower of a petition in bankruptcy or under state insolvency laws;
- filing of an involuntary petition against the borrower under bankruptcy or insolvency laws;
- breach of conditions relating to other indebtedness of the borrower to the lender;
- breach of other conditions and covenants set forth in the loan documentation;
- breach of any representation or warranty under the loan documentation or in the borrower's application for a loan; and
- default under other obligations for borrowed money by the borrower to other lenders.

The borrower's counsel usually attempts to restrict the scope of the events of default and will seek to negotiate a grace period during which the lender can cure defaults under the loan documents.

The lender's remedies for default by the borrower include the right to accelerate the indebtedness and foreclose the mortgage and take other actions against the collateral tendered by the borrower as the lender deems appropriate. Typically, the provisions with regard to remedies affirmatively state that the lender may take such actions as it deems appropriate in its sole discretion.

The lender may also waive the exercise of its remedies upon the occurrence of default, without prejudice to its rights to bring an action on the occurrence of later defaults. As with the note, the borrower is required to waive rights to such legal formalities as may be required by state law to the extent that such legal formalities are waivable under local law.

## ■ Summary

This Chapter covered common loan documents used by commercial real estate lenders, such as the following:

- Guaranty
- Loan commitment
- Security agreement
- Title insurance policy
- Certificate of borrower
- Completion/repair agreement
- Assignment of leases and rents
- Replacement reserve agreement
- Assignment of management agreement
- Agreement to amend, comply, or correct

An in-depth presentation of key documents (the promissory note and the mortgage) were presented. The promissory note evidences the borrower's obligation to the lender. The mortgage provides the lender with a security interest in the borrower's real property.

The title and lien theories were reviewed. These two legal theories outline the nature of a lender's interest under the mortgage. Under the title theory, the lender has actual title to the mortgaged property until the mortgage loan is repaid. Under the lien theory, the lender has only a security interest against mortgaged property, rather than a true title interest.

## ■ Chapter 5 Review Questions

1. Match the description to the appropriate term.

   a. Guaranty

   b. Promissory note

   c. Mortgage deed of trust

   d. Loan commitment letter

   _____ Provides the lender with a security interest in borrower's real property as collateral for the debt

   _____ Memorializes the lender's offer to make the loan and summarizes the essential terms of the transaction

   _____ Evidences the borrower's obligation to the lender and sets forth the essential terms of the borrower's obligation

   _____ Documents a promise by a third party (e.g., an affiliate or principal of the borrower) obligating the third party to pay the obligation of the borrower in the event of default under obligation to the lender

2. All of the following documents are commonly associated with commercial real estate loans EXCEPT

   a. escape clause.

   b. assignment of leases and rents.

   c. replacement reserve agreement.

   d. assignment of management agreement.

3. Check three critical issues to consider when drafting a guaranty.

   _____ A waiver of subrogation by the guarantor

   _____ A clear statement that the lender has the right to proceed against the borrower

   _____ A clear statement that the lender has the right to proceed against the guarantor

   _____ Identification of the receipt of adequate consideration on the part of the guarantor

4. The incremental value of a _____ guaranty versus a full guaranty may vary by the state law of a given jurisdiction.

   a. cash

   b. limited

   c. collateral

   d. net worth

5. Match the description with the appropriate term.

   a. Interest

   b. Maturity

   c. Capacity

   d. Prepayment

   _____ Interest rate to be charged by lender on the outstanding principal balance of the loan

   _____ Outlines whether and under what conditions the borrower may prepay all or a portion of principal

   _____ Something the borrower must demonstrate in order to enter into the obligation and make a note enforceable

   _____ Date on which all the outstanding principal and accrued interest owed to the lender by the borrower is payable

6. Check all that apply to multiple borrowers and the joint and several liability of a promissory note.

   _____ Each borrower should appear as a maker on the note.

   _____ Borrowers are not equally liable for the entire amount of indebtedness of the note.

   _____ Each borrower is liable for the entire amount of indebtedness of the note.

   _____ Borrowers are jointly and severally liable for the entire amount of indebtedness of the note.

7. The commercial mortgage contains a number of representations and warranties by the borrower with regard to the property and the borrower's status. Common representations and warranties provided by borrowers in a commercial mortgage include all the following EXCEPT

   a. borrower has title to the property subject to certain permitted encumbrances.

   b. delivery of the mortgage may conflict with existing agreements made by the borrower.

   c. no additional consents of third parties are required for the delivery of the mortgage.

   d. delivery of the mortgage does not conflict with any existing agreements or laws to which the borrower is subject.

8. Check all provisions common to a mortgage.

   _____ Condemnation

   _____ Estoppel certificates

   _____ Restrictive covenants

   _____ Conditions for leasing the mortgage property

   _____ Lender's right to books and records of the property

   _____ Default and remedies outlining provisions of borrower's default

9. Under the title theory of mortgage, the mortgagee's title gives them the right to immediate possession of the mortgaged property in the event of loan default.

   a. True

   b. False

10. Which of the actions listed below can a lender take in the event of a default under an obligation secured by a deed of trust?

    a. Begin litigation

    b. Take immediate possession of the property

    c. Execute the lender's security interest in the property

    d. Compel the trustee to sell the property in satisfaction of the obligation

# Commercial Loan Servicing

### learning objectives

*Upon completion of this chapter, you should be able to*

- identify general conditions of the commercial loan servicing function;

- differentiate aspects of the cycles and activities of the commercial loan servicing function;

- list common tasks performed by the loan servicer;

- recognize components of key reports related to loan servicing; and

- determine essential concepts connected with loan servicing activities.

## ■ Introduction

The commercial loan servicing function commences the day the loan is closed, and continues until the note and security instruments are satisfied through payoff, foreclosure of collateral, or other legal remedies. The loan servicer may not be the same entity that originated the loan because loans are often sold either individually or in pools to outside private and institutional investors. As discussed previously, investors include banks, savings and loans, insurance companies, pension funds, and government-sponsored agencies.

Whether the servicing is performed directly by the investor or by an outside contract servicer, the overall objective is to manage the real estate mortgage in accordance with the documents and requirements of the investor, for the life of the loan, and protect and preserve the security interest of the note holder. This Chapter looks at the activities of the commercial loan servicer.

Commercial loan servicing administration can be divided into the following cycles and activities:

- New loan setup and file maintenance
- Payment application, remittance, and reporting
- Escrow and reserve administration
- Collateral inspection, monitoring, and preservation
- Transfer of ownership, subordinate financing, partial releases, easements, seizures, and condemnations
- Default administration
- Annual auditing and reporting requirements
- Servicing transfers, purchase acquisitions
- Master servicing

## New Loan Setup and File Maintenance

### Servicing File

It is important that most of the documents processed, underwritten, and executed at closing are delivered to the commercial loan servicer as soon after closing as possible, usually within a few days. Most commercial real estate mortgage loans require monthly repayment installments. Prior to the first mortgage billing or payment date, the servicer must

- inventory the loan documents;
- construct a servicing file; and
- enter the loan into the computerized servicing system.

### Loan Setup

The servicing file should contain most of the loan origination and underwriting documentation. Also included are copies of the note, mortgage, and all other security, escrow, and collateral agreements executed at closing by the borrower. The original note and security agreements are held in safekeeping by the servicer, investor, or outside document custodian.

Once the commercial loan documents are inventoried and the servicing file has been assembled, the loan is entered into the servicer's computerized loan servicing system. All necessary information is either put into the system directly from the source documents or from manually prepared setup sheets. Information should include the following:

- Loan terms
- Borrower
- Investor
- Collateral
- Escrow

Larger pools of loans acquired through structured transactions or bulk acquisitions may be more efficiently set up through electronic downloading or tape-to-tape transfer. Under any method of system setup, a comprehensive edit must subsequently take place to ensure that all required fields are complete and accurate.

### File Maintenance

Because most commercial loan servicers maintain hard copy loan servicing files, it is a good idea to maintain a backup copy of all critical documents. This is typically accomplished by microfiche, microfilm, or optical image of documents at an off-site location in the event of a natural disaster.

## ■ Payment Application, Remittance, and Reporting

The mortgage payment, cash remittance, and periodic reporting cycle entails

- monthly collection, transfer, and disbursement of cash; and
- reconciliation and reporting of all activity processed by the servicer.

This includes any loan installment billing or mortgage coupon generation or ordering required.

### Account Maintenance: Monthly Payments

The servicer must establish appropriate custodial accounts for the deposit of funds collected and maintain strict control of all such funds held in trust. All accounts and related records should be maintained in accordance with the loan documents, applicable servicing agreements, and sound accounting and banking practices. These accounts should be insured and usually require a minimum rating from a recognized bank rating agency.

Separate accounts are typically established for the following:

- Principal and interest (P&I)
- Taxes and insurance (T&I)
- Replacement reserves
- Completion escrows
- Other special reserves or holdbacks

Many servicers also routinely use receipts-clearing bank accounts to clear daily deposits, as well as disbursement-clearing accounts from which remittances are channeled.

Ordinarily, the borrower's monthly payment consists of

1. interest;
2. principal; and
3. escrow deposits for servicer-paid taxes and insurance.

### Account Maintenance: Additional Fund Requirements

Commercial loans originated over the last several years increasingly require that the borrower include additional funds with the monthly installment to be held and disbursed by the servicer for ongoing repairs, replacement, and maintenance. The payment may also include late charges and other amounts required to fund escrow shortages or to repay advances made by the servicer on the borrower's behalf.

It is the servicer's responsibility to

■ post the installment to the borrower's account; and

■ ensure that the funds are properly transferred and credited to the appropriate bank account.

Most sophisticated commercial loan servicing systems track bank balances and generate bank transfer advices and transaction reports. These reports are used to reconcile accounts. Payment shortages and overages are handled in accordance with the loan documents and servicing agreements, which are usually very specific on the topic.

### Remittance (PITI and Advances)

The servicer must periodically remit collection of principal and interest, minus service fees, based on agreed upon schedules, to all outside investors. Principal, interest, and other income collected on portfolio loans serviced by the investor are credited internally to investment and revenue accounts.

The servicer may be required to advance scheduled principal and interest on delinquent loans to the investor. This is usually the case for

■ loans that have been pooled as collateral for a mortgage-backed security (MBS);

■ collateralized mortgage obligation (CMO); and

■ real estate mortgage investment conduit (REMIC).

These may include advances made to pay taxes, insurance, and property preservation on behalf of the defaulted borrower. They are recovered through

■ reimbursement process with the investor;

■ liquidation of the real estate; and

■ mortgage insurance claim.

### Reporting

The computerized commercial mortgage servicing system tracks all borrower and property level activity and balances. Most servicing systems have the capability of generating

■ standardized borrower, investor, banking, collateral, and activity reports on a periodic basis; and

■ customized reports (as necessary).

An important part of the commercial loan servicing cycle is the production, reconciliation, and distribution of reports detailing loan related information and activity. Investors require specific reports at certain times during the month as well as at year-end. The servicer is also obliged to provide the borrower with periodic reports relating to:

■ interest payments;

■ rate adjustments;

- escrow balances; and
- property inspections, etc.

Contractual requirements may demand that the servicer also supply reports to:

- government regulators and agencies, mortgage insurance companies, rating agencies; and
- other outside interested parties.

# Escrow and Reserve Administration

This area of the commercial loan servicing operation accounts for and disburses funds for taxes, insurance, property repairs, and maintenance. The funds held were either

- accumulated from the borrower as part of their periodic payment; or
- were deposited at the inception of the loan.

Funds may also have been deposited for disbursal as a result of an insurance claim, condemnation, or eminent domain settlement.

### Escrow Department

The escrow department is responsible for

- paying bills as they come due; and
- making any necessary advances in the event of an escrow or reserve shortage to protect the interest of the lien holder.

Escrow shortages and overages must be recovered and reimbursed in accordance with the loan documents and applicable local law.

The servicer must keep accurate records of the status of all taxes and assessments that could become a lien against the property, making certain that all such bills have been paid before penalties are assessed. It is also important that adequate hazard, flood, liability, rent loss, and other insurance coverages be placed and maintained on the properties. Most investors have specific limits, endorsements, and deductibles for each type of coverage and require the servicer to obtain or force place insurance if the borrower cancels the policy or defaults on the premium.

### Escrow Analysis

At least annually, the servicer must compute the required escrow payment based on reasonable estimates of assessments and bills to determine that sufficient funds are being collected to meet all escrow payments. This is commonly referred to in the industry as an *escrow analysis*. It is usually performed after the first real estate tax payment of the year.

If, as a result of performing an escrow analysis, the amount held by the servicer together with the future monthly installments of escrow exceeds the amount required to pay escrow items as they become due, the excess is either

- reimbursed to the borrower; or
- credited against future escrow payments.

Any escrow shortage identified by the escrow analysis should be recovered as quickly as the loan documents allow, but certainly prior to the next scheduled escrow disbursement that would create a cash shortage.

### Non-Escrowed Loan

If the security instrument or applicable law does not provide for the collection of escrow, the servicer should obtain evidence that all taxes, assessments, insurance premiums, ground rents, and other charges have been paid. This can be accomplished by requiring the borrower to furnish proof of payment in the form of a receipt or cancelled check, or by using some other reliable means of verification. Servicers can usually obtain tax payment information either directly from the tax authority or through a tax service company.

If the servicer discovers a delinquent tax assessment or insurance premium on a non-escrowed loan, the servicer should make demand on the borrower to pay the item and provide proof of payment prior to any penalty or event of risk (insurance cancellation, tax sale) to the property.

In most servicing arrangements, the servicer is required to advance the escrow payment when a shortage exists and either recover later from the borrower, or in the event of foreclosure, through the property liquidation or insurance/guarantee claim process.

## ■ Collateral Inspection, Monitoring, and Preservation

A periodic inspection of the mortgaged premises and a review of the income and expense statements for the property's operational activities are important tools in anticipating and preventing default.

### Property Inspection

The on-site visit by the servicer or the servicer's fee inspector helps the servicer to

- evaluate the quality and upkeep of the buildings, fixtures, and chattel; and
- assess the effect of changes and competition in the property's market area.

The servicing agreement or guide generally determines the frequency and extent of the property inspection. The security documents usually permit the note holder and the designated servicer access to the property, and provide remedies if such reasonable access is denied or information is withheld.

It may be necessary to perform a property inspection as a result of an event of default or prior to a foreclosure sale to determine the condition and marketability of the real estate. Also, the lender may not wish to take title to the property if serious environmental concerns exist that may create liability to the servicer. An inspection may also be called to confirm the completion of certain repairs or construction required as a result of a completion or replacement reserve agreement, or as a result of a natural disaster.

### Income and Expense Statement Review

The servicer should obtain and review operating and financial statements for the property in conjunction with the periodic inspection. These statements, provided and certified by the borrower or property manager, can be collected by the inspector in the field or mailed to the servicer when completed.

Most borrowers are on a calendar year end for tax purposes and close their books as of December 31. Investors, recognizing the benefit of reviewing a full year's financial activities, require audited or certified statements to be submitted and reviewed within three to five months of year end. If this does not coincide with the inspection date, interim operating statements may be annualized.

In either event, it is important that the formal property inspection report include an analysis of the performance of the property as a business that generates cash. It is from the cash revenue that the loan is repaid and the collateral maintained and improved.

Most commercial loan security documents require annual, and often quarterly, financial statements. Most servicers are now equipped to electronically capture and store key operating and financial data in the servicing system for analysis and monitoring purposes. Key ratios and trends are thus readily available for query, comparison, and manipulation from property to property and from year to year.

Anything unusual or questionable should be discussed with the borrower and fully documented in the file or formal report. Concerns identified during the review of the financial statements often require follow-up or corrective action by the borrower to return the property to compliance with the loan documents. Situations or variances that negatively impact income and the debt coverage ratio usually entail vigilant monitoring, additional inspections, and investor notification.

### Inspection Report

Because of the importance placed on the property inspection, many investors require the use of their own standardized inspection reports, specifying what to inspect and request, as well as how to document observations and inquiries. The inspector should use checklists and questionnaires, and take many photographs as well as copious notes.

The formal report is rarely prepared in the field, so the inspector must be able to draft a written report based on his or her memory and any documentation collected or produced while at the property. The report should provide general information about the property, including the following:

- Name
- Address
- Borrower
- Property manager
- Date of inspection
- Loan number
- Overview and rating of the property's overall condition and marketability

The attributes and amenities that the inspector should review and comment on vary from property type to property type. Generally, the review should include the following:

- Building condition and structural integrity
- Common areas, lobbies, atriums, and entryways
- Condition of fixtures and chattel property
- Landscapes, fences, walls, sidewalks, and parking lots
- HVAC, plumbing, electrical, gas, and boilers
- General condition of interior units and suites
- Security, fire extinguishers, smoke detectors, and lighting
- Environmental issues
- Street and rail access, loading docks, and public transportation
- Lease and rental market and trend analysis
- Amenities
- Deferred maintenance
- Review of leases, vacancies, turnover, unleasable space, and down units
- Neighborhood and area market conditions

## ■ Transfer of Ownership, Subordinate Financing, Releases, Easements, Seizures, and Condemnations

During the life of the loan, the servicer may be required to process, approve, and execute changes in certain provisions and conditions in the original loan documents, as a result of a borrower initiated request or because of external conditions impacting the real estate.

These transactions and changes may or may not have been specifically contemplated in the original loan documents, so good judgment and knowledge of local laws and customs are important.

In any event, the servicer should protect the security position of the investor by adhering to the servicing agreement, contract, or guide that addresses the activity.

### *Transfer of Ownership (Loan Assumption)*

Many security instruments allow the sale or transfer of the mortgaged property subject to the approval of the servicer and/or investor. This provides the new owner with the benefits of the terms of the existing loan, which may include

- lower-than-market interest rate; and
- reduced financing charges paid at closing.

The servicer requires that the borrower and potential buyer provide information about the transaction and the creditworthiness of the buyer and the ability to manage the property. The loan assumption is then processed, underwritten, and either denied, approved, or approved, with conditions. Once the transaction is approved and any conditions met, the transfer and assumption closes and the new borrower's liens are recorded at the courthouse.

If the servicer receives a loan assumption request or any information that a change of ownership has occurred, he or she should determine if the security instrument contains any due-on-sale provisions. A due-on-sale clause generally means that if the mortgagor sells, transfers, or in any way encumbers the property, then the mortgagee has the right to implement an acceleration clause making the balance of the obligation due.

The unauthorized transfer of a loan containing a due-on-sale clause is usually defined as a nonmonetary default in the security instrument. The servicer should consult with the loan documents and servicing agreements for guidance as to enforcement.

## Subordinate Financing

The commercial real estate mortgage or deed of trust that is being serviced is usually a first lien position in the real estate. The original property financing may have also allowed for subordinated debt or second liens. A different servicer usually services the additional loans, which are satisfied only after the first lien in the event of collateral liquidation.

The servicer may also be called on to review and approve secondary financing requests by the borrower that are allowable under the terms of the first mortgage or deed of trust. In the absence of any specific underwriting criteria in the loan documents, the servicer should process and underwrite in compliance with investor instructions. Ongoing monitoring of secondary loan performance is an important indicator of property cash flow problems and potential default.

If the security instrument has a due-on-encumbrance provision and a subordinate lien has been placed against the property, the servicer should determine if an event of default has occurred. Any unauthorized lien may trigger a nonmonetary default clause of the security instrument. Again, the servicer should consult the loan documents, servicing agreements, and local law for guidance as to enforceability.

## Releases

Loan security instruments often contain provisions permitting borrowers to request a partial release of the collateral. The servicer may be required to analyze and approve the release as a result of a(n)

- voluntary request from the borrower; or
- eminent domain or condemnation action instituted by a government authority.

A borrower may request a partial release for various reasons, such as to improve, to change the use of, or to sell the portion of the real estate being released. In any event, it is important for the servicer to understand what is motivating the borrower in order to make the appropriate decision.

The borrower should supply certain information whenever a substantial portion of the mortgaged property is to be released. Such information usually includes a description of the collateral, surveys, appraisals, independent inspection, contracts, plans, and permits evidencing a transfer or construction project, and any required title endorsement.

The servicer must determine what effect the release may have on the value on the balance of the secured real estate. Many investors require a paydown of the loan before any partial release is considered.

### Easements

Commercial real estate is often subject to easements. An easement is a right or an interest that one property owner has in the land of another. This benefit is either one of land ingress or egress (appurtenance) or in gross, such as a public utility easement.

Servicer and/or investor approval is usually required before the borrower may grant any easement that may depreciate the value of the original collateral. Title company consent or endorsement is also necessary, since the easement will alter the legal description and survey on which the original title policy was issued. A new survey, as well as a review by the local zoning board, may be required depending on the size and nature of the easement.

### Seizure

Various federal statutes provide for the civil or criminal forfeiture of certain types of real estate used or intended to be used to commit or to facilitate the commission of certain violations of federal law. A criminal forfeiture can occur when a property owner is convicted of a covered violation, while a civil forfeiture can occur when the property is used in connection with certain criminal offenses. The U.S. Marshals Service takes possession of the property and is responsible for notifying all interested parties. The recorded security instrument should provide the name of the lien holder for any seized property in the servicer's portfolio.

Most lenders rely on the *innocent lien holder* defense in such seizures, which provides that lien holders are protected if they can prove that the alleged violation occurred without the lien holder's knowledge or consent. Innocent lien holders will be paid out of the liquidation proceeds if the seizure is confirmed. It is imperative that the servicer control and monitor all proceedings and actions relating to forfeiture and seizure.

### Condemnation

A condemnation occurs when the government takes private property, through eminent domain rights, for public use. Some form of fair compensation is usually paid to the property owner when this occurs. Most security instruments address this possibility and provide that the borrower

- notify the servicer of any condemnation action;
- authorize the servicer to participate or take action during condemnation proceedings; and
- assign borrowers interest in any condemnation proceeds to the servicer.

## ■ Default Administration

Commercial loan security instruments and servicing agreements are written to provide the servicer with as much ongoing information as possible to allow the servicer to monitor and analyze property activities. This is so that the servicer can identify potential problems before they occur. For example, future delinquencies may be foreseen and perhaps prevented by inspecting the property or reviewing operating statements.

Preventive maintenance on potential problem loans is critical to a successful commercial loan servicing operation because foreclosure, workout, and restructuring activities are extremely labor intensive and costly.

### Monitoring Commercial Loans

Because commercial real estate loans are inherently more complex than single-family, consumer, or most non-real estate commercial loans, a variety of factors influence delinquency. Most delinquencies are caused by one or more of the following:

■ Inexperienced, ineffective, or disinterested ownership or management

■ Improper or uncontrolled financial operations and cash management

■ Limited financial resources of borrower

■ Misjudgment of or unforeseen change in the rental market

■ Misjudgment of or unforeseen change in expenses

■ Functional obsolescence of property

■ Generally depressed local economy

■ Deliberate disregard for obligation

Prompt and accurate identification of the cause of a problem loan is imperative if the servicer intends to mitigate the impending default. Many sophisticated services maintain a watchlist of loans for the purpose of closely monitoring otherwise current loans with potential property, borrower, or market problems. The extent to which a servicer can become directly involved in the day-to-day activities of the property operation in such a situation is usually limited until an actual event of default, either monetary or nonmonetary, occurs.

### Delinquency/Collection

Most commercial real estate loan installments are due on the first day of each month. This means that the loan is technically past due on the second day. However, payments are typically received throughout the entire first two weeks of the month because late charges are not assessed during the payment grace period as defined in the note. When the servicer can actually accelerate the loan and initiate a foreclosure action depends on the timing of any notices required and/or remedies available in the security instruments. The servicer should contact the borrower within several days after the usual payment remittance date to determine the borrower's intentions.

Occasional delinquencies are common but can be tolerated only under genuinely distressed conditions. Chronic delinquencies are serious and suggest a more systemic cause and require a more deliberate solution or action. Late charges and default interest normally are not very effective in enforcing collection, although the additional fees, if paid, do help offset the increased costs associated with servicing delinquent accounts. Late charges that are assessed must be collected from the mortgagor separately. They usually cannot be deducted from regular loan payments, escrows, or other reserves. Late charges may remain outstanding and paid only as a result of a payoff or liquidation.

The servicing agreement requires the servicer to notify the investor of the default and outline the specific action to be taken or recommended. Many investors reserve the right to approve or initiate default activities themselves. The servicer is usually required to

- perform a property inspection and financial analysis of the property within a few months of the default; and
- provide the investor with a report of condition and plan of action.

If the borrower cannot or will not immediately bring the loan current, the servicer must either pursue a workout or refer the loan for foreclosure.

### *Workouts*

The servicer must first determine how much flexibility and autonomy the investor allows in restructuring the loan. Many servicing agreements do not allow or severely restrict the options available to the servicer. Some investors prefer to approve each action or handle the workout directly.

Given that the servicer has the authority to act on behalf of the outside investor, several remedies are available. Many of these remedies can be used in combination. All require the full cooperation of the borrower and a sincere intent to cure the default.

Any workout plan should be in writing and predicated on a pre-negotiation letter. Reinstatement proposals could include several of the following actions:

- Capitalization and deferral of arrearages
- Reduction of interest rate
- Payment moratorium
- Reduction of payment amount/negative amortization
- Forgiveness, reduction in loan amount
- Interest-only payments
- Infusion of cash by borrower
- Release of reserves, impounds
- Supplemental loan for improvements or to fund operating loss
- Cash flow mortgage

Note that these potential solutions address the terms of the note and security instrument and not the operation and management of the property. Strong monitoring and some business involvement on the part of the servicer are essential in the overall plan to cure.

Loan workouts and modifications can often return a nonperforming loan to current status, but may fail in the long run and simply delay the inevitable foreclosure. As compensation for the agreement to restructure or forbear, it is advisable to require that the borrower

1. put up additional collateral;
2. provide a personal guarantee; and
3. provide some other form of security.

Loan workouts are typically of limited duration and are intended to provide temporary relief to a borrower experiencing cash flow problems.

### Foreclosure

Foreclosure should be pursued or recommended when the terms of any loan restructure are not being met and all other means of collection have been exhausted. Once the loan has been accelerated and any required notice of default delivered to the borrower, the foreclosure proceeds along one of two paths—judicial sale or power of sale. The type of foreclosure depends on the requirements of the state where the property is located.

### Judicial Sale States

In a judicial sale state, foreclosure is initiated by filing a complaint in the county where the property is located. The complaint will

■  identify the nature of the default;
■  reference the security instrument; and
■  state the amount of arrearages.

Future action is administered by the court and includes serving all interested parties, providing any notices, receiving answers to the complaints, and reviewing discovery documentation. Foreclosure in these states can take anywhere from several months to several years depending on local laws, procedures, and court backlog. The process can be shortened if no disputes exist and a summary judgment is issued, but it can be lengthened if the case goes to trial or the judge orders mediation.

### Power of Sale States

In power of sale states, the foreclosure process is expedited through a sale of the property by the servicer on behalf of the investor or trustee pursuant to the security instrument. This is a nonjudicial process. Notices are posted and/or given to the borrower and all interested parties identifying the default and the servicer's/trustee's intention to foreclose. The servicer calculates the gross amount of outstanding arrearages and usually bids that amount at the public foreclosure sale. The proceeds from a third party foreclosure sale or subsequent asset sale by the servicer are used to satisfy liens in priority order.

A foreclosure on real estate generally is conducted to foreclose on personal property that is covered by the security agreement section of the security instrument. In some situations, the tangible personal property covered by the mortgage or deed of trust may be different from that described on the Uniform Commercial Code (UCC) security agreement. In some cases, it may be advisable to foreclose on the personal property without foreclosing on the real estate. In either case, it is important to follow the applicable state version of the UCC, plus the terms of the mortgage or deed of trust.

In some situations, the borrower and servicer may agree to the borrower's granting a deed to the servicer reconveying some or all of the real estate covered by the security instrument. This *deed-in-lieu* has the effect of avoiding the costly and time-consuming judicial and nonjudicial foreclosure process. Although this procedure expedites recovery of property, it does not extinguish or allow termination of junior liens and encumbrances, and the transfer is more susceptible to later attack by a junior lien holder or under a subsequent bankruptcy.

### Bankruptcy

There are three types of bankruptcy proceedings with which the loan servicer may become involved in connection with a defaulted commercial real estate loan. They are Chapter 7, Chapter 11, and Chapter 13.

**Chapter 7.** Chapter 7 is a straight liquidation of the company or assets to satisfy creditors. The filing is usually involuntary, initiated by creditor petition, and supervised by a court or creditor-appointed trustee.

**Chapter 11.** Chapter 11 is a reorganization of the company and allows the borrower to produce a plan to reinstate all or a portion of outstanding debts. The court may appoint a trustee to manage the property or allow the servicer to step in as "debtor in possession."

In a reorganization plan under Chapter 11—the most common form of bankruptcy involving commercial real estate—the borrower is required to work with creditors to produce a feasible repayment schedule that can be confirmed by a majority of the creditors. This may involve:

■   changes in creditors' rights;

■   a cramdown of debt; and

■   distribution of assets as compensation for debt.

Creditors submit a proof of claim listing all secured and unsecured debts with the borrower. The amount of any debt that exceeds the value of underlying collateral is considered unsecured. The borrower's disclosure statement must set forth all necessary information provided by the creditors and address how and when all debts will be satisfied. If agreeable to the creditors by vote, the court will confirm the plan and the appointed trustee will monitor compliance with the plan.

**Chapter 13.** Chapter 13 is the reorganization of individual regular income. The borrower's secured and unsecured debts must not exceed certain limits to qualify under this filing. Chapter 13 allows the debtor to keep encumbered assets in return for devoting a portion of future income to outstanding debt over a limited period of time.

**Automatic Stay.** Under all filings, an automatic stay is placed that protects the borrower against creditor judicial action and foreclosure sales. The stay remains in place throughout the proceeding unless relief is granted or the bankruptcy is dismissed. The servicer can request the stay be lifted on the grounds that there is no equity in the assets or because of lack of protection of the creditor's interests. The stay can also be vacated if it can be shown that the property is not essential for a successful reorganization.

Most bankruptcy courts recognize that if a bankruptcy petition has been filed for an improper purpose or in *bad faith*, the automatic stay may be lifted to permit prompt foreclosure or the case may be summarily dismissed.

# Annual Auditing and Reporting Requirements

### Auditing Requirements

Most servicers are subject to an annual review of their financial condition and servicing operations by an independent auditor and/or regulatory agency examiner. Some investors rely on a certified public accountant (CPA) audit performed in accordance with the Uniform Single Audit Program as promulgated by the Mortgage Bankers Association of America. The CPA opinion that is issued as a result of this audit provides investors, guarantors, insurers, and rating agencies, among others, with assurance that the servicer is performing its responsibilities properly. Institutional investors and guarantors, such as Fannie Mae, Freddie Mac, HUD, Ginnie Mae, and the Resolution Trust Corporation employ their own examination teams and subject the servicer to periodic audits and site visits.

Servicing agreements usually require the servicer to certify annually that it has performed specific duties stipulated in the agreement. These duties include, but are not limited to

- paying real estate taxes;
- ensuring that hazard insurance is adequate;
- performing property inspections; and
- reviewing operating statements.

The servicer is also required to submit its own financial statements and evidence of fidelity and errors and omissions insurance coverage as well. It is important for investors and other interested parties to determine annually that the servicer is financially responsible and capable of making servicing advances, repurchasing loans, and generally meeting obligations that come due.

### Reporting Requirements

The servicer has certain annual borrower and IRS reporting responsibilities as well. Each January, IRS Form 1098, detailing the borrower's calendar year interest charges, must be sent to the borrower and, in summary form, to the IRS. Other reports such as IRS Form 1099, Form 1099A, and escrow statements may also be required.

# Servicing Transfers, Purchase Acquisitions

The stated servicing fee annuity to which the servicer is entitled is often considered owned by the servicer. The servicer may have the contractual right to the fees by virtue of having

1. originated the loan;
2. an assignment of the servicing; or
3. actually purchased the servicing rights.

Many servicing agreements allow the servicing rights to be sold or simply transferred from one servicer to another.

Usually, the terms and conditions under which the loans are serviced for the investor remain unchanged and, typically, the investor reserves the right to approve the sale or transfer. Operationally, when a transfer occurs, the new servicer must be prepared to quickly receive, set up, and edit new loan files and data.

# ■ Master Servicing

Master servicing can be defined as the collection and reconciliation of information and funds from various subservicers for dissemination and remittance to the investor. This also includes the monitoring of subservicer activities to ensure that prudent commercial mortgage loan servicing is performed in accordance with all applicable loan documents and servicing agreements.

The subservicer is a lender that performs the ongoing servicing activities for the mortgage or pool under an agreement with the contractually responsible servicer.

Master servicing can result from an investor's desire to funnel borrower reporting and remittance activity through one master servicer for control purposes, or a structured transaction.

## Structured Transaction

In a structured transaction, groups of mortgages are arranged in pools that constitute a mortgage-backed security (MBS). Payments from the borrower collected by the subservicer are remitted to the master servicer, who aggregates the funds for pass-through to the investor, usually through a trustee. Both subservicer and master servicer deduct service fees, as specified in the various contracts, from the interest portion of the payment. Other fees, such as guarantee fees, custodial fees, and fiscal agent fees, may also be deducted from the gross interest to arrive at the scheduled pass-through interest to the investor.

Most multiple class MBS transactions are issued as public or private Real Estate Mortgage Investment Conduits (REMIC). A more flexible mortgage security structure than its predecessor, the Collateralized Mortgage Obligation (CMO), the REMIC was created by the Tax Reform Act of 1986. The REMIC expanded the appeal and availability of the CMO structure to a wider investor base and provided for preferred tax treatment for issues and investors. The master servicer typically reports and remits to a trustee in this type of transaction.

## Role of the Master Servicer

The role of the master servicer varies significantly from the responsibilities for full or direct serviced loans. The master servicer, for example, has little, if any, direct contact with the borrower or the collateral. Direct servicing activities are delegated or contracted to the subservicers, such as responding to borrower requests, property inspections, tax and insurance disbursements, and collection calls. The master servicer is usually required to advance scheduled principal and interest and make servicing advances on defaulted loans. This responsibility may initially reside with the subservicer, but, at some point, is usually transferred to the master servicer for final liquidation, accounting, and reimbursement.

# ■ Summary

This Chapter addressed the loan servicing function, which starts at loan closing and continues until the note and security instruments are satisfied. The cycles and activities of the commercial loan servicing were discussed in detail and include the following:

- ■ New loan setup and file maintenance
- ■ Payment application, remittance, and reporting
- ■ Escrow and reserve administration
- ■ Collateral inspection, monitoring, and preservation
- ■ Transfer of ownership, subordinate financing, partial releases, easements, seizure, and condemnation
- ■ Default administration
- ■ Annual auditing and reporting requirements
- ■ Servicing transfers, purchase acquisitions
- ■ Master servicing

The tasks and requirements of loan servicers in performing the activities and cycles of commercial loan servicing were identified throughout this Chapter. Some of these include the following:

- ■ Inventory of documents and setup of servicing files
- ■ Establishing appropriate custodial accounts for the deposit of funds collected
- ■ Posting and crediting installments to the borrower's account
- ■ Requiring periodic reports from borrowers
- ■ Maintaining accurate records of the status of taxes and assessments
- ■ Conducting escrow analysis
- ■ Performing property inspections and formal reporting
- ■ Monitoring loan performance for potential default
- ■ Collecting late charges and developing workout plans

Three types of bankruptcy—Chapters 7, 11, and 13—were also briefly discussed.

The overall objective of the servicing function was presented, which is to manage the real estate mortgage in accordance with the loan documents and requirements for the life of the loan and to protect and preserve the note holder's security interest.

# ■ Chapter 6 Review Questions

1. Check the two statements that reflect the overall objective of the loan servicing function.

   _____ To protect and preserve the borrower's security interest

   _____ To protect and preserve the note holder's security interest

   _____ To manage the real estate in accordance with local and state regulations

   _____ To manage the real estate mortgage in accordance with the loan documents and requirements for the life of the loan

2. Investor loan servicing requirements often conflict with the servicing terms detailed in individual loan documents.

   a. True

   b. False

3. Match the description with the appropriate loan servicing cycle or activity.

   a. Master servicing

   b. Loan setup and file maintenance

   c. Escrow and reserve administration

   d. Payment application, remittance, and reporting

   e. Collateral inspection, monitoring, and preservation

   _____ Servicing operations that account for and disburse funds for taxes, insurance, property, repairs, and maintenance

   _____ Collection and reconciliation of information and funds from various subservicers for dissemination and remittance to the investor

   _____ Monthly collection, transfer, and disbursement of cash and the reconciliation and reporting of all activities processed by the servicer

   _____ Periodic inspection of the mortgaged premises and a review of the income and expense statements of the property's operational activities

   _____ Process of inventorying commercial loan documents, setting up the servicing files, maintaining hard copies of all files, and backup of critical documents

4. Match the description with the appropriate term.

   a. Workouts

   b. Easements

   c. Condemnation

   d. Escrow analysis

   e. Unsecured debt

   f. Due-on-sale provision

   _____ Debt that exceeds the value of underlying collateral

   _____ A right or an interest that one property owner has in the land of another

   _____ The breakdown of the required escrow payment based on a reasonable estimate of assessments and bills to determine that adequate funds have been collected to meet all escrow payments

   _____ Alternative action to foreclosure for the benefit of the lender and borrower; includes loan modification and various forms of forbearance

   _____ Occurs when the government, through eminent domain rights, takes private property for public use. Fair compensation is normally paid to the property owner

   _____ A provision, typically associated with the unauthorized transfer or encumbrance of property, the result of which is that the balance of the loan obligation becomes due as a consequence of the unauthorized activity

5. In the administration of mortgage payments, the loan servicer must establish appropriate custodial accounts for the deposit of funds collected and maintain strict control of all such funds held.

   a. True

   b. False

6. Check four activities commonly performed by the loan servicer in conjunction with on-site property inspections.

   _____ Conduct due diligence reviews.

   _____ Employ the use of checklists and questionnaires.

   _____ Review the general interior and exterior of the building.

   _____ Take photographs and notes for later use when writing the formal report.

   _____ Write a formal report that includes general information about the property.

7. Each January, an IRS form reflecting the borrower's calendar year interest charges must be sent to the borrower. That form is

   a. IRS Form K-l.

   b. IRS Form 1098.

   c. IRS Form 1099.

   d. IRS Form 1140.

8. Borrowers must report certain information whenever a substantial portion of mortgaged property is released. The borrower's reports should include all of the following EXCEPT

   a. title endorsement.

   b. independent inspection.

   c. reports of civil forfeiture.

   d. a description of the collateral.

   e. contracts, surveys, and appraisals.

   f. plans and permits evidencing transfer or construction project.

9. Match the description with the appropriate term.

   a. Judicial sale

   b. Power of sale

   _____ Type of foreclosure proceeding used in some states that is handled as a civil lawsuit and conducted entirely under the auspices of court

   _____ A provision in a deed of trust or mortgage that empowers a trustee, without court order, to sell property in the event of default by the mortgagor and to apply the proceeds of the sale to satisfy the obligation, the costs of invoking the procedure, and the expenses of the sale

10. Match the description to the appropriate term.

    a. Chapter 7

    b. Chapter 11

    c. Chapter 13

    _____ Bankruptcy filing which gives a trustee power to distribute a debtor's assets to creditors

    _____ Where an individual debtor files a budget with the court and agrees to make partial payment to auditors over a limited period of time, also called the "wage earner plan"

    _____ A reorganization of the company that allows the borrower to produce a plan to reinstate all or a portion of outstanding debts; court may appoint a trustee or allow the servicer to act as "debtor in possession"

# Commercial Development: Meeting New Challenges

## learning objectives

*Upon completion of this chapter, you should be able to*

- identify growth control regulations and techniques used to enforce them;

- recognize regional planning efforts designed to counter the negative impacts of development efforts; and

- list the main emphasis and goal of the Community Reinvestment Act.

## ▪ Introduction

In the early 1990's, *Business Week* magazine published a special issue entitled "Reinventing America—Meeting the New Challenges of a Global Economy." It discussed

- the "mind-numbing cost" of rebuilding domestic infrastructure;

- issues of public safety, affordable housing, public education, retraining workers impacted by corporate downsizing and defense base closures;

- the need for structural reforms of Glass-Stegall Act barriers; and

- the need for more "bite" in the Community Reinvestment Act of 1977 to encourage banks to play a more active role in the solutions to these issues.

Recurring themes in this special *Business Week* issue were the innovations being employed to meet these challenges. Of particular significance here are those initiatives that affect commercial, mixed use, and infrastructure developments undertaken in the 1990s, and the renewed emphasis on public/private partnerships and other ventures available to finance such development.

This Chapter explores some causes of the increasing conflicts resulting from local growth control regulations, municipal annexations, and other competition for revenues, and approaches to overcome them. It also explores the demands on the development community, mortgage bankers, and local government planning and finance officials working together to meet the challenges of a global economy as well as changing environmental standards and monitoring regulations.

# ■ Growth Control Regulations

The objectives of growth control regulations and techniques for enforcement and implementation vary widely. For example, caps are frequently imposed on commercial and residential development to limit new construction until necessary public facilities and service improvements are made available through developer exaction, impact fees charged to pay for public improvements and services, and appropriate public finance vehicles. Growth control measures of this type are usually implemented through interim control ordinances, moratoria, and conditions imposed upon zoning, subdivision, and other land use and building approvals.

Growth control objectives encourage the following:

■ Utilizing existing facilities

■ Conserving open space and preventing sprawl

■ Avoiding or mitigating environmental impact

■ Preserving the character of a community or historic or cultural features

■ Improving housing opportunities

Growth control legislation must meet the test of bearing a reasonable relationship or "nexus" to a legitimate public purpose in order to avoid taking private property without payment or compensation.

Subject to the constitutional limitation on municipal and county police powers (articulated by the U.S. Supreme Court in *First English Evangelical Lutheran Church of Glendale v. County of Los Angeles, Nollan v. California Coastal Commission,* and more recently in *Lucas v. South Carolina Coastal Council* and *Dolan v. City of Tigard),* local governments increasingly look to the development community to solve growth-related problems by exacting fees, dedications of right-of-way, and other contributions for (or participation in) public works, social and educational programs as a condition of obtaining development approvals and permits.

Enforcement and implementation techniques include the following:

■ Use of restrictive covenants or other agreements

■ Transfer of development rights

■ Municipal annexations

■ Development agreements

■ Capital programming

■ Public acquisition

■ A variety of zoning, overlay, and special district techniques

In an effort to find cheaper land and avoid some of the burdens attendant to development adjacent to urban centers, many residential builders in the 1980s purchased and developed land in rural and remote areas. This increased commuting time for new homebuyers because the homes were farther from places of employment. This kind of urban decentralization and job/housing imbalance has become a major cause of traffic congestion and air pollution.

## ■ Regional Planning Efforts

Because the impact of development does not stop at municipal boundaries, there has been increasing pressure for some form of regional oversight in an effort to deal with the impact. Voluntary cooperative efforts have been organized as councils or associations of governments, often referred to as COGs. Two examples in California are

1. Southern California Association of Governments (which includes 6 counties and 126 cities); and
2. Association of Bay Area Governments (which includes 9 counties and 91 cities in northern California).

Although bolstered by legislation to provide long-range transportation planning, these California COGs have no direct land use control authority other than attempts to have regional land use policies implemented through local land use control programs of the member governments.

Florida has enacted regulation to evaluate large-scale expansion through development regional impact legislation. It requires any development having an impact beyond the boundaries of the local government in which the project is proposed to construct roads and pay fees representing the *proportionate share* of public facilities necessary to mitigate such impacts.

Still another approach to regional planning and finance is the use of legislation such as California's Joint Exercise of Powers Act, which includes the ability of authorities created pursuant to the Act to issue revenue bonds. Joint Powers Authorities will play a major role in addressing some of the jurisdictional as well as financing issues in the reuse of property impacted by recent military base closings.

Following is a recent example of an effort to provide a regional solution to environmental impacts on a bird species, the California gnatcatcher. The gnatcatcher was listed as a "threatened" species under the federal Endangered Species Act and a proposed rule was introduced to establish a pilot program to monitor the bird.

Under the new rule, an environmental panel developed criteria to allow local governments and landowners to assemble sufficiently large habitat areas, through purchase, dedication, or condemnation, to provide regional sanctuaries for the gnatcatcher. Local governments enrolling in the program exact fees (and land dedication of sufficient size and habitat value) from development projects which would affect the threatened species. The fees are used to pay the cost of acquiring and maintaining the land required to provide habitat for the gnatcatcher. Compliance with the program is not exclusive—in other words, a permit for an "incidental take" of the threatened species will still be available under other provisions of the Act.

This pilot program was supported by U.S. Interior Secretary Bruce Babbitt as a means of avoiding another "train wreck"—a reference to the much publicized clash over the spotted owl by timber interests and environmentalists in the Northwest.

In anticipation of the listing of the California gnatcatcher as a threatened species, some creative planners and environmentalists working together on a project in Carlsbad designed around the problem. First, they planned meaningful habitat corridors for the gnatcatcher. They then proposed a draft Habitat Conservation Plan to maintain the habitat and open space areas to be restricted for the gnatcatcher. Lastly, they set up development around the habitat corridors. This approach allows the proposed development to meet and use either the criteria of the pilot program or the existing provisions of the Endangered Species Act, whichever best suits the timing of the project.

Legislation prohibiting impacts on the environment and conservation of specific resources are numerous and include the following:

- The Federal Clean Air Act and regulations adopted by regional air quality management districts
- The Federal Clean Water Act (in particular, Section 404 regulating the discharge of dredge or fill materials into waters of the United States which include wetlands)
- The Federal Water Pollution Control Act and state water quality regulations

Other entities, including coastal commissions, mountain conservancies, and agencies such as the San Francisco Bay Conservation and Development Commission, as well as state land agencies, the U.S. Forest Service, and the Bureau of Land Management also play major roles in planning and permitting development and use which impacts the land and other resources under their jurisdictions.

Projects impacting the environment and conditions imposed to monitor impacts, along with measures to protect or mitigate against such impacts, are developed through environmental impact reports and environmental impact statements, referenced below.

## ■ Environmental Regulations

In the past, developers have been frustrated by the cost and resulting delays from efforts to comply with the environmental impact analysis and disclosure requirements of the National Environmental Policy Act (NEPA) and the California Environmental Quality Act (CEQA). Of particular concern are project opponents who demand that alternatives be explored before any development decision is reached. However, developers who want to obtain the coordinated and/or internally consistent approvals and findings required by governmental agencies ultimately find an ally in legislation like NEPA, California's CEQA, and Florida's DRI regulations.

This prediction is based on a number of factors. Initially, the environmental impact statements and reports required by NEPA, CEQA, and Florida's DRI legislation may provide the only *glue* or means to coordinate and force consideration of major project elements by the agencies from which approvals must be obtained.

In addition, well located, thoughtfully planned projects which address local and state needs and which are supported by solid science and procedurally sound administrative records are more likely to gain the support of local governments. More importantly, they allow the findings upon which approvals must rely to be more confidently and readily made. Government officials responsible for development approvals are becoming increasingly aware of newly emerging regulations that require the imposition of mitigation monitoring and reporting programs. Coupled with annual reviews typical in development agreements, they know that approval will be subject to scrutiny for a long time.

The U.S. Forest Service, in an effort to streamline planning required under the National Forest Management Act, prepared an extensive multivolume analysis and critique. In it, further support is provided for the emergence of such an approach, as well as recent case law and NEPA amendments. It makes it clear that the environmental review and assessment process, while frequently involving polar opposite positions, is in the final analysis a *process* intended to force considered decisions about a project. If a project is to be approved, the appropriate agency must find it to be supported by a procedurally sound administrative record and by good science.

Finally, proponents of major commercial and mixed use development, as well as municipal and other public agencies, are increasingly using intensive community workshops or *charrettes* to obtain public input on development or reuse of strategically located land, districts, or areas before any site specific proposals are put forth. Workshops or charrettes are frequently conducted in coordination with local planning officials, well-known members of the architectural profession, and community activists. The input and data arising from these workshops provide an excellent guide to the scope and studies needed to support a preferred alternative to a proposed development.

# ■ Community Reinvestment Act of 1977

As provided in the regulations promulgated under the Community Reinvestment Act of 1977 (CRA), national banks, state member banks, and insured state non-member banks are all encouraged to help meet the credit needs of the local community, including low-income and moderate-income neighborhoods. They are to provide credit in the form of

- residential loans;
- housing rehabilitation loans;
- small business loans;
- farm loans;
- community development loans; and
- commercial loans.

They are also encouraged to periodically report on how their current efforts are helping to meet community credit needs in a CRA statement. The CRA statement is reviewed at least annually by the board of directors of each bank, and files on CRA activities are available for public inspection.

The special *Business Week* issue described at the beginning of this Chapter was followed in February of 1993 by a series of interagency "questions and answers" published by the Federal Financial Institutions Examination Council in an effort to help financial institutions meet their responsibilities under the CRA and increase public understanding of the CRA regulations.

In March of 1993, an article in the publication *Governing* described President Clinton's proposal for new community development banks. On July 15, 1993, there was a presidential announcement of CRA reform issues, and the next day the Office of the Comptroller of the Currency proposed new rules for national banks to make investments in community development corporations (CDCs) and community development projects (CDs). The reason, initially, was to implement provisions of the Depository Institutions Disaster Relief Act of 1992. The purpose articulated in the rule making proposal, however, was broader in scope:

> *The purpose of the requirement for community involvement in CDC and CD projects is to insure that the public welfare is the primary focus of these investments on a continuing basis and that these undertakings are not primarily for the benefit of bank investors. This requirement also promotes the partnerships between the community, bank and governmental leaders essential to CDC or CD project success.*
>
> *The dedication of CDC and CD project investment profits to public welfare activities would also insure that the primary focus on public welfare activities is sustained over the long term.*[1]

While the CRA requirements are really directives to the financial institution supervisory agencies—and do not require the regulated institutions to make any specific loans or to make below market interest rate loans or other loans inconsistent with safe and sound lending—it appears, at least from the perspective of one member of the Federal Reserve Board, that the regulated financial institutions have not been doing enough.

Reflect for a moment on the needs arising out of the hurricane damage in the South, the flooding in the Midwest, and the fires and earthquakes in California, as well as the fiscal crises facing state and local governments. It can be expected that the new community development corporation and project investment rules will be complementary to the changes being proposed in the CRA regulations. There will be a real convergence of the interests and goals of government finance officials, financial institutions, and the development community resulting from these bank regulatory changes.

In President Clinton's July 15, 1993, message to Congress, which was accompanied by his proposed "Community Development Banking and Financial Institutions Act of 1993," the President stated it was his intention that the regulatory changes in the CRA would in fact complement the community development finance institution initiative so as to replace paperwork with performance oriented standards and facilitate increased community development activity by mainstream and community development financial institutions.

Reading between the lines of earlier policy statements made by the President and by Vice President Gore in "Technology for America's Economic Growth, a New Direction to Build Economic Strength" (February 22, 1993) might have suggested a number of the new changes in the Omnibus Budget Reconciliation Act of 1973 that should also prove complementary to this convergence. Among these changes are the following:

■ The permanent extension of the Qualified Small Issue Bonds provisions of Section 144 of the Internal Revenue Code with respect to manufacturing facilities

---

[1] Federal Register, July 16, 1993; and see final rule amending the Community Development Corporation and Project Investment Regulations 58 Federal Register 68464 (December 27, 1993)

- The permanent extension of the Qualified Mortgage Bond provisions of Section 143 of the Code to benefit first time homebuyers

- The adoption of recreational user fees for entrance into national recreation areas, monuments, and properties under the jurisdiction of the Bureau of Land Management, including areas of concentrated public use, boat launching facilities, campgrounds, etc.

- A tax credit for contributions to certain community development corporations

- The Empowerment Zone and Enterprise Zone community provisions

All changes were enacted as part of the Omnibus Budget Reconciliation Act of 1993.

## Public/Private Partnerships

Although public/private bargaining to address community needs has been in practice for a long time, the approach seemed to gain momentum in the 1970s. It has been suggested that this momentum started with the enactment of the National Environmental Policy Act in January of 1970. Land use planning and development approvals became far more restrictive after the enactment of major state and federal environmental laws, coastal zone management Acts, and ultimately, tax revolt legislation, such as California's Proposition 13.

While public/private partnerships emerged and became popular in many urban developments, the source of much of the renewed interest in this approach appears to be due to several factors:

- Lengthy discussion and call for this approach in the legislative history of the Intermodal Surface Transportation Efficiency Act of 1991 (ISTEA)

- Executive Order 12803 signed by former President Bush on April 30, 1992, describing his "privatization initiative"

- Establishment of the National Infrastructure Corporation pursuant to ISTEA (to provide for credit enhancement for infrastructure, among other matters)

In light of initiatives currently proposed by the Clinton administration, it is likely there will be a major expansion in the use of public/private bargaining and public/private partnerships to address the challenges of growth control, necessary public improvements and environmental regulations well into and beyond the 1990s.

In addition to the proposed fully automated 10 mile development of SR 91 in California's Orange County, similar projects are planned or have been approved in Arizona, Colorado, Florida, Georgia, Minnesota, Missouri, Texas, Virginia, and Washington. The financing is driven by user fees, including fees which increase during peak hours of congestion. The toll road fees are all monitored, controlled, and billed through a transistorized device the size of a computer diskette. Highway Patrol officers enforce laws through receipt of signals from the same device that a negligent driver has driven by.

Reactions to the proposals continue to be mixed. Some suggest that more emphasis is needed on public transportation and similar alternatives. It is anticipated that the increasing role of user fees will reduce traffic congestion, shorten commuter time, and reduce air pollution to standards consistent with federal and regional air quality levels. Recent filing for relief under the Federal Bankruptcy

Act will slow the progress of Orange County's toll road financing, but the delay is likely temporary.

Development proposals must anticipate user fees support public debt financing, or the use of a public/private partnership approach. Proposals must always address the long-standing policy of requiring the most "bang for the government buck." This policy will continue as a major element of any negotiations for economic development assistance, including those under the new Enterprise Zone and Empowerment Zone legislation.

Water quality proponents were pleased with the June 1993 enactment of the Water Pollution Prevention and Control Act of 1993. The Act modifies funding requirements and expands the range of water quality projects eligible for financing through state revolving funds.

The Environmental Protection Agency State Revolving Fund (SRF) program replaced the Construction Grants Program. The key element in the SRF approach is revolving loan payments, which provide assistance to additional recipients. The EPA views the program as a significant step in restoring the responsibility for financing waste water treatment facilities to states and municipalities.

An example of a public/private partnership approach to "reinventing" government is the May 1993 completion of the 15-story Nicholas Petris building, which is the new headquarters for the California Department of Transportation in Oakland. Under the arrangement, the state made incremental monthly progress payments to a subsidiary of a major financial institution that assumed the financial risk for design and construction. It set up an incentive system of bonuses and penalties, assuring on time delivery.

Working through the Office of Project Development and with an exemption from the (usual and slower) capital outlay building process, this design/build/fast track approach resulted in delivery of the completed building 13 months ahead of schedule and substantially under budget. There were savings to the state, including consolidation of personnel from five other sites. Consequently, it is expected that this kind of public/private design/build process will be used again.

## ■ Lessons from the Past

Most lenders working their way through OREO portfolios in the early 1990s learned the cost of leaving land use strategies to their borrowers rather than having their own experienced land use counsel. These have been hard lessons to learn. Sometimes thousands, even millions, of dollars in municipal reimbursements were made directly to a borrower for oversizing public improvements financed with bank loan funds. In many cases, unexonerated surety bond exposures were inadvertently assumed for incomplete improvements when taking back collateral.

Other lenders learned that one or two escrows closed in a single-phased project far too large for realistic absorption triggered homeowner maintenance obligations on all the unsold lots. Others learned that there was no easement or other access for use of common facilities or amenities in a multi-phase or mixed use project. In any case, the experience has not been a happy one.

The cost of credit extension for real estate has clearly gone up. This is a result of the adoption of minimum capital ratios which are fully phased in, the publication of new appraisal guidelines, and the letter of credit exposures no longer "off balance sheet." There is and will continue to be a real premium on finding the most cost-efficient, intelligently planned, risk sharing structure to assist banks in their role of addressing the development needs of their communities. Prodded by CRA reforms and the newly enacted Community Development Bank legislation, banks have to play this role. It is no longer a question of enticing banks to participate.

The lessons described above and techniques to avoid similar problems in the future are becoming familiar to bank credit and OREO officers. Financing commercial, mixed use, and public infrastructure and facilities becomes much more complex as we go forward. Common practices and techniques will involve the following:

- Use of public/private partnerships
- Structured and/or project finance techniques
- Familiarity with constitutional and other limits on the ability of state or local governments to raise debt in the tax exempt markets
- Awareness of securitization and refunding opportunities and even the use of swaps and swap derivative opportunities

## ■ Geographical Information Systems

Computer technology made possible the explosion in securitization and the emergence of sophisticated financial instruments and derivatives to hedge interest basis and foreign exchange exposures. Technology has also given rise to digitized electronic mapping and images and more sophisticated techniques for land use planners to detect and analyze trends, demographic changes, lending practices, traffic patterns, and smaller and smaller trace elements of contaminants.

These innovations in mapping and geographic information systems (GIS), computer assisted design, and other computer applications in land use planning and environmental assessment give local, regional, state, and national governments the ability to

- evaluate impacts on infrastructure, water quality, air quality, housing stock, etc.; and
- demonstrate impacts much more persuasively than possible in the past.

Indeed, these innovations may require the courts and legislators to take a new look at "linkage" issues.

Technology also increases the pressure on development proponents to embrace the NEPA and CEQA and Florida's DRI legislation as a means of coordinating and achieving consistent multi-jurisdictional review and approval of projects.

In addition, technology is likely to increase the use of the public/private partnership approach to

- negotiate the most cost-efficient risk sharing methods of meeting local needs;
- use monitoring programs to regularly review the basis for project approvals; and
- where necessary, make appropriate changes and adjustments.

## ■ Libraries, Culture, and the Arts

Increasingly, there appears to be more recognition of the valuable contribution of the arts and libraries, universities, historical and cultural buildings, and the more frequent involvement of local art councils and tourism bureaus as part of community planning and economic development efforts.

## ■ Statutory Versus Structured (De Facto) Vesting

Development agreements and other statutory vehicles arose out of a need to vest rights to build major phased projects without the risk of changes in zoning and land use regulations. These statutory protections provided lenders and their customers some much needed help in dealing with late vesting rules, as those established in California in *AVCO Community Developers, Inc. v. South Coast Regional Commission*.

Some non-statutory but effective "de facto" vesting means include

- public financing and the increasing use of project finance;
- structured capital market techniques; and
- public/private partnerships.

Revenue bond financing, benefit assessment financing, and community facilities district (CFD) financing (such as authorized by California's Mello-Roos Community Facility Districts legislature)—all have an inherent need to keep in place the revenue generating asset or the individual payers who collectively provide the debt service on such bonds. Whether or not credit enhanced, the underlying structure, public purpose, reliance, and expectations of property owners and lenders, primed by the first lien priority of such benefit and CFD financing, provides a type of de facto vesting.

An additional example of de facto vesting results from subdivision regulations that prohibit local planning officials from reducing densities in projects subject to community facility financing where the reduction in the number of lots or homes would decrease the number of homeowners or end users who are the intended payers of the debt service in CFD financing to the possible disadvantage of bondholders. This is not to say that such structured or de facto vesting provides the same kind or degree of protection or level of predictability against future land use changes as are available in statutory vesting vehicles. However, the development community and bankers should be aware of such de facto vesting and the opportunities to structure or thread such protection through any development approvals being sought.

## ■ RFPs and Beauty Contests

The request for proposal (RFP) process, as well as design contests and the so-called "beauty contest" approach used in San Francisco and elsewhere, continue to be used by municipalities to initiate development that addresses major urban issues or special district issues. Any repeat of the design/build/fast track public/private partnership approach like that used for the construction of California's Department of Transportation headquarters building in Oakland previously described will likely be the subject of an RFP process. This assures a similar level of financial integrity and skill of the private sector partner and of the individuals actually responsible for the organizational, scheduling, and operational details needed for timely delivery of such a facility.

## ■ Some Financing Examples

Most state and local governments possess a broad variety of public finance authority, for example:

- ■ Tax increment financing in community redevelopment
- ■ Housing revenue bonds
- ■ Lease revenue bonds
- ■ Certificates of participation

The use of community facility districts like that authorized by California's Mello-Roos legislation, with the broad range of public facilities that can be financed under such legislation, has grown dramatically (although not without controversy) in comparison to the special benefit districts and improvement districts previously relied upon for infrastructure improvements.

The availability of any particular public finance vehicle depends in large part on whether the

- ■ bond counsel for the issuer is comfortable with the structure;
- ■ public agency involved has the interest and political will to use the financing for the public purpose involved; and
- ■ financial consultant and underwriters involved (as well as the issuer) are satisfied that the financing is feasible and at an interest rate that works for all concerned.

Subject to convincing the public finance team in each case, recent legislative incentives suggest an increase in the public financing structures available to meet current financing challenges.

By an example that is only partly theoretical, consider (particularly with the approval of the North American Free Trade Agreement) a plant expansion where the facility and its output are dedicated to export with trade financing tied to an Eximbank loan or guaranty program. Initial profits are pledged to repayment of bond financing used to finance the expansion.

Another example is a development agreement with a county to use future sales tax subventions generated from a new job creating facility to pay debt service on assessment bonds sold by the county to provide funds to construct street improvements required for access to a new facility. If, as a result of some unforeseen calamity (flooding, fire, etc.), the county does not appropriate amounts equal to the sales tax subvention received in any given year and apply the same to debt service, the development agreement can provide that a county funded community development loan would be reduced dollar for dollar by payments made by the facility owner to pay debt service on the assessment bonds.

Suffice to say, lenders involved in innovative financing must fully understand and examine each and every element of a project and anticipate the risks involved. Banks and other lending institutions should be able to avoid the earlier described OREO lessons if they fully understand the following:

■ Land use components, applicable environmental regulations, timing, and flexibility needed to respond to adjustments required as a result of mitigation monitoring programs

■ New legislation

■ Changes in interest rates

■ Municipal budgeting and appropriation limitations; public finance capabilities

■ Best management practices and construction techniques

Lenders should also be alert to the securitization and secondary market opportunities and appropriate hedging opportunities.

## ■ Sustainable Development

Most planning officials are being exposed to the growing calls for *sustainable development,* and there is little doubt that increasing impacts on the environment and the regulatory requirements will, over time, force most development into compliance with the principles of sustainability.

With accelerating demands for increases in job opportunities and focus on infrastructure development, concerns have been raised that environmental regulations should be relaxed. While some relaxation may occur in the short run, sustainability teaches that the regulations need not be relaxed due to the fact that sustainable projects incorporate and address the mandates of environmental regulations.

Improved site selections that avoid obvious impacts on environmental resources and site planning and phasing strategies that are consistent with public financial resources and realistic absorption rates are becoming more common.

Obviously, increases in density and the use of mixed use projects, lofts, and other techniques assist in urban and suburban projects. This is not to imply that mixed use projects are easy to do. They are not. But the tools and the need exist and with some creativity, innovations in this area are bound to increase.

The concept of sustainable development is both simple and complex. Following are some common guidelines:

■ Place projects in locations where they will do the most long-range public good.

■ Plan around the environmental parts.

■ Consolidate densities through mixed use development near established transit nodes or to create new ones.

■ Build close to libraries and educational and cultural facilities.

■ Include day care.

■ Encourage small business.

Achieving progress in implementing sustainable development will not be an easy task. However, the environmental and fiscal pressures described in this lesson, coupled with the public/private partnership approach and some new and innovative use of existing financial and land use techniques, provide assistance.

## ■ Attribute Capture and Value Capture

From a land use planning prospective, it is likely that municipal, county, and regional planners will continue to identify major attributes within their jurisdictions—whether educational, cultural, recreational, tourism, nature, or transportation related. Municipal planners and finance officers will increasingly focus on those attributes (particularly those within, or within the general control of, the public sector) that form a part of each jurisdiction's historic, natural, competitive, or proximal advantage.

Obvious efficiencies can be achieved by

■ not stretching limited public resources to continue remote development;

■ providing appropriate density bonds and other incentives to encourage location of projects closer to jobs, schools, etc. (thereby avoiding some of the traffic generated impacts of remote development); and

■ utilizing suggestions made by the MegaCities Project.

Through community redevelopment techniques and others, there is likely to be an increase in the "capture" of properties that embody or are adjacent to major municipal attributes; for example, those with long-range renewable revenue generating potential available through a ground lease or privatization. Also likely is an increase in the so-called *third wave* strategies of promoting quasi-private organizations and community colleges to provide economic development services, training, and retraining.

Closely related to this concept of attribute capture is the concept of value capture in the form of revenue potential from secondary real estate development opportunities resulting from and adjacent to public/private infrastructure development.

Local government attribute capture and value capture are only part of a process that could be employed to reverse patterns of sprawl and the attendant draining of public revenues to respond to the requirements of developers searching for cheaper land in remote areas. Reversing such patterns will require long-term planning and some form of amortization of investment based on expectations for remote development that does not contribute to, or promote, the historic, natural, competitive, or proximal advantage needed to achieve long-term sustainability.

## ■ Summary

Well located, intelligently planned projects that address local community needs and are supported by solid science and procedurally sound administrative records will most easily gain development approvals. With the new financial incentives and techniques described in this Chapter, the renewed popularity of public/private partnerships as well as the increasing needs of state and local governments to find ways of improving public infrastructure and services, there seems to be a convergence of a number of old and new financial techniques. There is increasing interest in innovative approaches needed to cope with the land use, growth control, and environmental regulations.

## ■ Chapter 7 Review Questions

1. Check five common techniques used to enforce growth control.

   _____ Call options

   _____ Zoning techniques

   _____ Public acquisition

   _____ Capital programming

   _____ Municipal annexation

   _____ Use of restrictive covenants

2. Caps are rarely imposed on commercial and residential development to limit new construction until the needed public facilities and service improvements are available.

   a. True

   b. False

3. Check two examples of voluntary cooperative efforts to establish required governance that deal with the negative impacts of development efforts.

   _____ Association of Bay Area Governments

   _____ California Environmental Quality Council

   _____ Southern California Association of Governments

   _____ San Francisco Bay Conservation and Development Commission

4. All of the following are examples of legislation designed for direct prohibition of impact on the environment and conservation of resources EXCEPT

   a. Federal Clean Air Act.

   b. Federal Clean Water Act.

   c. National Forest Management Act.

   d. Federal Water Pollution Control Act.

5. Which statement is NOT true about Community Reinvestment Act requirements?

   a. CRA requirements are really directives to financial institution supervisory agencies.

   b. CRA requirements require that regulated institutions make loans that are below market interest rate loans.

   c. CRA requirements do not require regulated institutions to make loans that are below market interest rate.

   d. CRA requirements do not require regulated institutions to make loans inconsistent with safe and sound lending practices.

6. Check the two statements that reflect the purpose of the requirements for community involvement in Community Development Corporations and Community Development Projects.

   _____ To ensure that investments are primarily for the benefit of bank investors

   _____ To ensure that investments are not primarily for the benefit of bank investors

   _____ To ensure compliance with the Depository Institutions Disaster Relief Act

   _____ To ensure that public welfare is the primary focus of investments on a continuing basis

## Chapter 1 Review Questions

1. *a.* True
2. *b.*
3. *a.*
4. Originating loans
   Underwriting loans
   Securing a loan commitment
   Developing a loan application
   Securing an engagement letter
   Managing a closing/postclosing
5. *b.*
6. Proposed loan terms
   A summary of capital costs
   A complete description of improvements
   Financial and biographical information on borrowers
   A thorough description of the neighborhood, area, city, and region in which the property is located.
7. *c.*
8. *e.*

## Chapter 2 Review Questions

1. *c.*
2. *a.*
3. *b.*
4. *a.*
5. *b.* False
6. *d.*
7. *a., d., b., c.*
8. *a.* True
9. *b., c., a.*
10. No precise agreement on the amount of future benefits
    Represents value of a property to the present or a prospective owner
    No precise agreement on the appropriate adjustment to value for waiting or for uncertainty

## Chapter 3 Review Questions

1. *c.*
2. *a.* True
3. Considering loan terms
   Conducting market research
   Requesting real estate information
   Quantifying credit and track records of borrowers
4. *g.*
5. *c.*
6. *c.*

7. Membership provides the opportunity to attend seminars.
Membership provides the opportunity to hear industry-specific lectures.
Membership provides the opportunity to meet and socialize with developers, lenders, and consultants.

8. *d.*

9. *c.*

10. Loan type
Property type
Proposed loan terms

## Chapter 4 Review Questions

1. *b., c., d., a.*
2. *b.*
3. Debt service
Land planning
Developer experience
Repayment of principal at maturity
4. *b.*
5. *d.*
6. *a.* True

## Chapter 5 Review Questions

1. *c., d., b., a.*
2. *a.*
3. A waiver of subrogation by the guarantor
A clear statement that the lender has the right to proceed against the guarantor
Identification of the receipt of adequate consideration on the part of the guarantor
4. *d.*
5. *a., d., c., b.*
6. Each borrower should appear as a maker on the note.
Each borrower is liable for the entire amount of indebtedness of the note.
Borrowers are jointly and severally liable for the entire amount of indebtedness of the note.
7. *b.*
8. Estoppel certificates
Conditions for leasing the mortgage property
Lender's right to books and records of the property
Default and remedies outlining provisions of borrower's default
9. *a.* True
10. *a., b., d.*

## Chapter 6 Review Questions

1. To protect and preserve the note holder's security interest
To manage the real estate mortgage in accordance with the loan documents and requirements for the life of the loan
2. *b.* False
3. *c., a., d., e., b.*
4. *e., b., d., a., c., f.*
5. *a.* True
6. Employ the use of checklists and questionnaires.

Review the general interior and exterior of the building.

Take photographs and notes for use later when writing the formal report.

Write a formal report that includes general information about the property.

7. *b.*

8. *c.*

9. *a., b.*

10. *a., c., b.*

## Chapter 7 Review Questions

1. Zoning techniques

Public acquisition

Capital programming

Municipal annexation

Use of restrictive covenants

2. *b.* False

3. Association of Bay Area Governments

Southern California Association of Governments

4. *c.*

5. *b.*

6. To ensure that investments are not primarily for the benefit of bank investors

To ensure that public welfare is the primary focus of investments on a continuing basis

**a piece** Refers to security classes (tranches) rated as investment grade for institutional investors; can also include the class rated BBB, as that is considered an investment grade for most regulated institutions; also called senior pieces.

**abatement (rental)** Reduction or elimination of rent payments for a specified period of time, usually granted by the landlord as an inducement to the tenant to enter into or to renew a lease.

**abatement (tax)** Reduction in real property tax granted by a taxing authority as the result of an appeal (in some jurisdictions, tax abatements may also be granted as an inducement for development or to attract or retain job-providing industries).

**ACES** Alternative Credit Enhancement Structure

**absorption rate** Rate at which vacant space is either leased or sold to users in the market place; usually expressed in square feet per year or, in the case of multifamily housing, number of units per year.

**acceleration clause** Common provision of a mortgage that allows the holder to demand the entire outstanding mortgage balance due and payable in the event of a breach of the mortgage contract.

**accident** Unplanned, unexpected, and undesigned event that occurs suddenly at a definite place. *See* occurrence.

**accounts payable** Money owed by a business to suppliers of goods and services; considered current liabilities on the balance sheet.

**accounts receivable** Money owed to a business for goods or services provided to customers; classified as current assets on the balance sheet, with a contra account for bad debts on receivables.

**ACH (Automatic Clearing House)** Computer-based facility for interchange of electronic entries between financial institutions.

**ACORD form** Form utilized by the insurance industry for use between an Agency and a Company for Organization, Research, and Development.

**actual cash value** Valuation of damaged property that allows for depreciation.

**ADA compliance** Compliance with the provisions of the Americans with Disabilities Act, which establishes minimum requirements for facilities with public access to accommodate physically handicapped persons.

**additional insured** Individual, business, or organization covered by a policy in addition to the named insured.

**admitted insurer** Insurance company licensed to do business in a certain jurisdiction.

**advances** Payments made by the servicer on delinquent loans; can be required for property protection, taxes, insurance, and foreclosure costs.

**agency securities** Securities issued by government or quasi-government agencies such as Fannie Mae and Freddie Mac.

**aggregate deductible** Provision whereby the policyholder agrees to self-assume the payment of claims incurred up to a specific amount or limit, with the insurer paying all claims after such limit is attached.

**aggregate limit of liability** Provision which limits the maximum liability of an insurer for losses in a given time period (usually 12 months); usually expressed in maximums per accident (or occurrence), with an aggregate for all losses in any one year.

**agreed amount** Agreement whereby the coinsurance clause is waived if the insured agrees to carry a specific amount of insurance which represents at least 90 percent to 100 percent of total values at risk; also known as *stated amount coinsurance.*

**agreed amount endorsement** Insurance endorsement used with a policy containing a coinsurance clause, which binds the insurance company to an agreement that the amount of insurance carried under the policy is sufficient to meet the requirements of the coinsurance clause in the policy (addition of the agreed amount endorsement eliminates the risk of the coinsurance penalty).

**all-cash offer** Proposal to purchase property without any contingency to obtain a loan to finance any portion of the purchase price.

**all-in cost** Term applied to the total costs of a securitization; usually quoted in basis points to reflect what the costs would have added to yield if they had not been spent on the creation of the security.

**amenity** Feature that enhances property value (i.e., off-street reserved parking within a condominium community, proximity of public transportation, tennis courts, or swimming pool).

**American Council of Life Insurance (ACLI)** ACLI collects data from life insurance companies regarding their portfolios; has information on approximately 87 percent of all mortgages held by life insurance companies.

**amortization** Repayment of a mortgage debt with periodic payments of both principal and interest, calculated to retire the obligation at the end of a fixed period of time.

**anchor tenant** Prime tenant in a shopping center, such as an established department store, which attracts the bulk of customers to the center.

**appraisal** Opinion or estimate of value; also refers to the process by which a value estimate is obtained.

**appraiser** One qualified by education, training, and experience to estimate the value of real and personal property.

**arm's length transaction** Transaction in which the parties involved are entirely independent of each other, deal with each other as strangers, and have no reason for collusion.

**asbestos** Insulating, fire-resistant, and heat-resistant material commonly used in insulation and roofing.

**assessment** Value factor assigned to real property and used to determine real property taxes; process of reaching the assessed valuation; also, an add-on tax to raise money for a special purpose.

**asset** Property or right owned, tangible or intangible, that has monetary value and is capable of providing future benefits to its owner.

**assignment of lease** Mortgage clause that passes control of leases on an income producing property to the lender; often a condition to making a loan to ensure, in the case of mortgage default, that any continuing income from the property goes directly to the lender.

**assignment of rents** Transfer to the mortgagee of the right to collect rents from tenants in the event of default by the property owner.

**assignment** Transfer of ownership rights, or interests in property, as in a mortgage, lease, or deed of trust.

**assumption** Buyer's acceptance of primary liability for payment of the existing note secured by a mortgage or deed of trust.

**assumption agreement** Written agreement by one party to pay an obligation originally incurred by another.

**assumption fee** Amount paid to a lender for the paperwork and processing of records necessary to approve and document a new debtor.

**attornment agreement** Letter acknowledging a new owner as a landlord or a new organization as a loan servicer.

**audit** Official examination and verification of bookkeeping accounts to prove the accuracy of figures and the adequacy of accounting controls; may be done by public accountants hired for this purpose or by a company's own employees (latter is called an *internal audit*).

**available funds** All funds available or collected including prepayments and servicer advances.

**B piece** Term applied to the classes (tranches) of CMBSs rated "BB" and lower; also called below investment grade (BIG) by regulated institutional investors.

**backup** Process of taking all data stored on the computer and copying it onto tapes, or another storage medium, so it can be shipped to another location for safe keeping.

**balance sheet** Report of the financial position of a business at a specific point in time, showing its assets, liabilities, and owner's equity.

**balloon mortgage** Mortgage with periodic installments of principal and interest that do not fully amortize the loan; balance is due in a lump sum at a specified date usually at the end of the term.

**balloon risk** The risk that a borrower is unable to make a balloon payment at maturity.

**bankruptcy** Court proceeding to relieve the debts of an individual or business unable to pay its creditors.

**base rent** Minimum fixed guaranteed rent in a commercial property lease.

**base stop** Maximum amount of building operating expenses that will be borne by the landlord prior to passing additional amounts through to the tenant; expressed as an absolute dollar amount or dollar per square foot amount.

**base year** Similar to base stop, except that rather than being specified as an absolute amount, the landlord's expenses are limited to the amount incurred in a specified calendar or fiscal year, usually (but not always) the calendar year in which the lease commences.

**basis point** 0.001 percent (one one-hundredth of one percent); used primarily to describe changes in yield or price on debt instruments, including mortgages and mortgage-backed securities.

**basis risk** Refers to the risk of the underlying mortgage loans and offered certificates tied to different indices; possibility of the certificate accruing interest at higher interest rates than the underlying mortgage loans (when the aggregate amount of interest on the certificates is greater than the collateral, the amount is known as the basis-risk shortfall).

**bid** Price at which a seller will sell particular securities; in the security and commodity trade, the highest price offered for a security or commodity at a given time; also, a "quotation or quote."

**binder** Legal agreement issued by the insurer or it's agent to provide evidence of coverage until such time as a full policy(ies) can be issued.

**bodily injury liability insurance** Protection against loss arising out of the liability imposed upon the insured by law for damages due to bodily injury, sickness, or disease sustained by third parties. *See* personal injury.

**boiler and machinery insurance** Coverage for the loss to boilers and machinery caused by explosion or mechanical breakdown; may cover damage to the boilers, machinery, other property, and business interruption.

**bona fide** Latin term meaning *in good faith,* without fraud.

**book value** Capitalized cost of an asset, less depreciation taken for accounting purposes, based on the method used for the computing of depreciation over the useful life of the asset; actual value of an asset after deducting depreciation and all liabilities is the net book value.

**borrower** One who receives funds in the form of a loan with the obligation of repaying the loan in full with interest.

**borrower/guarantor full recourse** Agreement wherein the borrower/guarantor has personally agreed to fully repay all amounts owed under a mortgage loan, irrespective of whether the collateral is adequate to retire the debt; gives the holder of the note, or other negotiable instru-

ment, the right to recover against the borrower/guarantor personally, including any and all assets of the borrower/guarantor.

**borrower/guarantor partial recourse** Agreement wherein the borrower/guarantor has personally agreed to repay a set dollar amount, all amounts exceeding a stated dollar amount, or a percentage of the outstanding balance of the mortgage loan; gives the holder of the note, or other negotiable instrument, the right to recover against the borrower/guarantor personally, including any and all assets of the borrower/guarantor, but *only* to the extent specified (for example, a borrower/guarantor may agree to pay the first $1 million of a $5 million loan or the top 25 percent of the loan).

**breakpoint** In a retail lease, the point specified in absolute sales dollars or sales dollars per square foot, above which the tenant has agreed to pay percentage rent in addition to base rent (for example, in addition to base rent, a tenant may agree to pay 2 percent of annual gross sales above $2 million; in this case, $2 million is the breakpoint).

**broad form** Term used to describe coverage which extends beyond "standard" peril insurance policies, i.e., fire and extended coverage, named perils, etc.

**broad form property damage** Endorsement to a general liability policy that grants expanded coverage to property in the care, custody, or control of the insured, property which is not normally insured if damaged by the insured's negligence.

**builder's risk insurance** Fire and extended coverage insurance for a building under construction. Coverage increases automatically as the building progresses and terminates at completion.

**building code** Regulations based on safety and health standards that govern design, construction, and materials used in construction.

**business interruption insurance** Compensation to a business owner or operator for income lost when the business is closed due to fire or any other insured hazard.

**call option** Provision of a note that allows the lender the right to demand or "call in" the balance of the obligation; can be exercised due to a breach of specified terms or conditions, or at the discretion of the lender (such as when the note rate is lower than the current market rate).

**CAM expenses** *See* common area maintenance.

**capital improvement** Any structure or component erected as a permanent improvement to real property that adds to its value and useful life.

**capital improvement reserves** Reserves may be required by loan documents to fund the future payment of capital improvement for the property.

**capitalization** Conversion of a future net income stream into present value by using a specific desired rate of earnings as a discount rate.

**capitalization analysis** Analysis based on the conversion of a future net income stream into present value by using a specific desired rate of earnings as a discount rate.

**capitalization rate** Rate of return on net operating income considered acceptable for an investor and used to determine the capitalized value; rate should provide a return or, as well as a return of, capital; also known as *cap rate.*

**cash flow (after taxes)** Cash received less cash paid out, including income taxes paid.

**cash flow (before taxes)** Cash received less cash paid out, before any consideration for income taxes.

**cash flow modeling** When pools of loans are converted to securities, all payments, including balloon maturities, are chronologically collated into a cash flow pool and then sequentially allocated to the various classes of securities created with the issuance of a CMBS.

**cash reserve** Reserves normally kept by the owner of the property to fund any operating shortfall or capital improvements that are required for the property.

**casualty or theft loss** Losses on property arising from fire, storm, theft, or similar sudden and unexpected occurrences.

**central business district (CBD)** Area geographically located within the central business district of a municipality.

**certificates of insurance** Form that evidences policy coverage, limits, etc., and is generally used as proof of insurance; has no legal status and cannot be used in lieu of actual insurance policies.

**claims made** Policies written on a "claims made" basis only cover claims presented during the particular year the policy is in force, for incidents which occurred during the same policy year, or for any previous year noted in the "claims made" policy (retroactive date); contrasts with an "occurrence" policy that responds to incidents regardless of when the claim is reported.

**closed (exclusive) listing** Right of one agent to be the only one, other than the owner, who may sell the property during a period of time.

**closed period** Interval of time under a mortgage during which the loan cannot be prepaid.

**closing** In real estate, the delivery of a deed, financial adjustments, the signing of a note, and the disbursement of funds necessary to consummate a sale or loan transaction.

**closing statement** Financial disclosure giving an account of all funds received and expected at closing, including escrow deposits for taxes, hazard insurance, and mortgage insurance (all FHA, VA, and most conventionally financed loans use a uniform settlement statement called the HUD-1).

**coinsurance** Clause which forces an insured to share in a loss if he/she is underinsured at the time of the loss; for a reduced premium, the insured is obligated to carry an amount of insurance to a specified minimal level, usually prescribed to be a fixed percentage of the value of the insured property; failure of the insured to insure to that level results in a penalty in payout equal to the amount deficient.

**collateral** Property pledged as security for a debt, for example, mortgaged real estate.

**collateral valuation process** Process by which a property's price is determined.

**commercially reasonable** Fair, proper, just, or suitable under generally accepted business (commercial) standards or circumstances.

**commingling** Combining funds (such as escrows) into one account that should be accounted for and deposited into separate accounts.

**commission** Agent's compensation for negotiating a real estate or loan transaction, often expressed as a percentage of the selling price.

**commitment** Agreement, often in writing, between a lender and a borrower, to loan money at a future date, subject to specified conditions; in secondary marketing, an agreement, in writing, between a lender and an investor to buy and sell mortgages under specific terms.

**common area** Area owned by the owners or tenants of a complex or subdivision, for the common use of residents.

**common area maintenance expenses (CAM expenses)** Expenses associated with the maintenance of the common areas.

**comparables** Properties used for comparative purposes in the appraisal process that have similar characteristics to the subject property; also, "comps."

**comprehensive general liability insurance** Policy that covers a variety of general liability exposures, including premises, property, and operations, products liability, owner's and contractor's protective, contractual liability, elevator liability, and employer's liability.

**concessions** Discount or other inducement given by a landlord or seller to a prospective tenant or buyer to induce them to sign a lease or purchase property.

**condemnation** Taking of private property for public use under the right to eminent domain with just compensation paid to the owner and others with an interest in the condemned property.

**consideration** Something of value offered and accepted in exchange for a promise, without which an agreement is unenforceable.

**constant** Percentage of the original loan paid in equal annual payments that provides principal reduction and interest payments over the life of the loan (for example, a $1 million loan with a 10.8 percent constant requires a $108,000 annual payment).

**construction loan** Short-term, interim loan for financing the cost of construction; lender advances funds to the builder at periodic intervals as work progresses.

**construction loan agreement** Written agreement between a lender and a builder and/or borrower that details the specific terms and conditions of a construction loan, including the schedule of payments.

**construction loan draw** Partial disbursement of the construction loan based on the schedule of payments in the loan agreement; also, "takedown."

**construction costs** All costs incurred in the completion of a construction project, including land, labor, overhead, and builder's profit.

**contingency** Clause in a contract that requires the completion of a certain act or the occurrence of a certain event.

**contingency reserve** Reserve account in which funds are held until certain specified conditions are satisfied.

**contract** Agreement between two or more parties that creates an obligation to do or not to do a particular thing.

**contractor** Person or company who agrees to do work and/or furnish materials for a contracted price; subcontractors are often hired by the contractor to perform specialized or technical labor.

**corporate resolutions** Affirmative and formal action by the board of directors of a corporation approving a transaction, activity, or decision.

**cost approach to value** Valuation approach in which the value of a property is determined by computing the replacement value of improvements, depreciation, and the value of land.

**cost overrun** Amount of money required or expended over and above budgeted cost, including such items as labor, interest, materials, and land.

**covenant** Legally enforceable promise or restriction in a mortgage; breach of covenant in a mortgage usually creates a default as defined by the mortgage, and can be the basis for foreclosure (for example, the borrower may covenant to keep the property in good repair and adequately insured against fire and other casualties).

**credit** Financial status--ability of borrower to meet the terms of his obligations.

**cross-defaulting clause** Clause in some mortgage agreements that states a default by the borrower on one mortgage loan also triggers a default on the other loan stated in the clause.

**current asset ratio** Ratio of current assets to current liabilities.

**cycle (economic)** Period of time, such as when the economy is growing or when it is in a recession.

**date-down title insurance endorsement** Instrument, provided by the title company, indicating that no liens have been placed on the property since its original issuance of the title insurance policy, or since any prior date-down endorsement.

**debris removal** A property policy extension of coverage that grants coverage for the expense of removing debris caused by damage to property by an insured peril; property should be defined as both insured and uninsured.

**debt/equity ratio** Proportion of capital borrowed to the amount of capital invested out-of-pocket or obtained through the sale of common stock; also, "leverage ratio."

**debt service** Borrower's periodic mortgage payments comprised of principal and/or interest on the unpaid mortgage balance.

**debt service coverage ratio** Ratio of effective annual net operating income to annual principal and/or interest payments; also, "debt service coverage."

**deed** Document by which title to real property is transferred or conveyed from one party to another.

**deed of trust** Type of security instrument in which the borrower conveys title to real property to a third party (trustee) to be held in trust as security for the lender, with the provision that the trustee shall reconvey the title upon the payment of the debt, and, conversely, will sell the land and pay the debt in the event of a default by the borrower. *See* mortgage.

**deed-in-lieu** Deed given by a borrower/mortgagor to a lender/mortgagee to satisfy a debt and avoid foreclosure.

**default** Breach or nonperformance of the terms of a note, the covenants of a mortgage, or the terms of other loan documents.

**default interest rate** Interest rate stipulated by certain mortgage documents which is triggered by a breach or nonperformance of the terms of a note, the covenants of a mortgage, or the terms of other loan documents.

**default letter** Letter sent to the borrower indicating that a breach or nonperformance of the terms of a note, the covenants of a mortgage, or the terms of other loan documents has occurred; also advises the borrower of the rights of the lender under the note/mortgage and requires that the default be cured.

**deferred maintenance** Postponed, infrequent, or inadequate maintenance practices on a building or property, often resulting in physical depreciation and loss of value; can be an indicator of inadequate cash flow or lack of pride in the property; also, "curable depreciation."

**delinquency** Failure of a borrower to make timely payments specified under a loan agreement.

**demand letter** Correspondence sent to the borrower indicating that unless the loan is made current within a certain time frame, the lender can, by virtue of a default, declare the entire principal balance outstanding as well as all interest due under the note to be due and payable.

**demand note/mortgage** Note or mortgage that the lender can call due at any time and without prior notice.

**demographics** *See* demography.

**demography** Study of the characteristics of human populations such as size, growth, density, distribution, and vital statistics.

**demolition clause** Coverage extended to cover the cost of demolishing property damaged by an insured peril; policies may be extended to cover the cost of demolishing undamaged property made necessary by a bylaw, court order, etc.

**density** Ratio between total land area and the number of residential or commercial structures placed upon it; local ordinances usually regulate density.

**depreciation** Decline in value of a building or other real estate improvement, resulting from age, physical wear, and economic or functional obsolescence; deducted annually from net income.

**direct payment** Method of payment wherein a check or other form of consideration is delivered directly to the investor's or servicer's place of business.

**disappearing deductible** Deductible that disappears as the loss gets larger, i.e., a $500 deductible will not apply to losses over $10,000.

**discount** In loan originations, refers to an amount withheld from loan proceeds by a lender; in secondary market sales, the amount by which the sale price of a note is less than its face value (in both instances, the purpose is to adjust the yield upward, either in lieu of interest or in addition to interest).

**discount rate** Rate of return used to convert expected future cash flows into present dollar value equivalent.

**discounted cash flow analysis (DCF)** Method of applying an appropriate discount to cash to be received in the future to arrive at the present value of those future earnings.

**distressed property** Term that denotes property in trouble due to one of several reasons, such as: cost overrun, insufficient income, poor management, or any other conditions that affect the mortgagor's ability to repay the loan on a timely basis.

**divest** To release an interest one has in property.

**down payment** Portion of the sale price paid a seller by a buyer to close a sales transaction, with the understanding that the balance will be paid at settlement; also, the difference between the sale price of real estate and the mortgage amount.

**draw** Periodic advances of funds according to the schedule of payments in a construction loan agreement; also "advance, disbursement, payout, progress payment, or takedown."

**due date** Date when the borrower must pay the interest and/or the principal due on his or her mortgage, as stated in the note, as well as any escrow payment.

**due diligence review** Examination by a purchaser of a servicing portfolio; generally the reviewer will look at credit quality and underwriting of the loan collateral underlying the servicing rights; correctness and completeness of the loan documents; the seller's servicing practices and methodologies; and the accuracy of the portfolio offering document (as used here, a reunderwriting of the loan in line with borrower's request to determine the feasibility of the request by lender).

**due-on-encumbrance** Provision appearing in a mortgage providing for the acceleration of a loan upon the placement of additional mortgage liens on collateral already pledged/mortgaged to a lender.

**due-on-sale** Clause in a mortgage stating that if the mortgagor sells, transfers, or in any way encumbers the property, then the mortgagee has the right to implement an acceleration clause making the balance of the obligation due.

**easement** Right to the limited use or enjoyment of land held by another, including, for example, an interest in land to enable sewer or other utility lines to be laid, or to allow access to a property.

**economic or commercial real estate weakness** Area exhibiting poor occupancies, low rents, plant or military base closings, or low sales and appraised values.

**economic value** Condition of the property based on its earning potential.

**effective gross income** Stabilized income after vacancy and bad debt allowances that a property is expected to generate.

**effective rent** Rental income generated by a lease computed over the life of the lease and expressed as an annual dollar amount or annual dollar amount per square foot; typically computed as the aggregate rent to be paid under the lease net of any abated rent and allowances, divided by the term of the lease.

**egress** To go out; used with the word *ingress* (to go in) to describe the right of access to land.

**encroachment** Improvement that illegally violates another's property or right to use that property.

**encumbrance** Anything that affects or limits the fee simple title to property, such as mortgages, leases, easements, or restrictions.

**engineer's report** Report rendered by an engineer stating the physical condition of property that has been inspected with a summation or recommendation thereof.

**environmental impairment insurance** Special form of insurance designed to protect an insured against claims for liability and clean-up costs related to pollution; may be granted for gradual and sudden and accidental pollution, and is always written on a claims made form.

**Environmental Protection Agency (EPA)** Agency responsible for enforcing environmental liability.

**equivalent level rent calculation** As opposed to *effective rent*, a method of calculating rent using a time-value-of-money approach; market discount rate is applied to all cash flows from the lease to obtain a present value that is then reduced by the cost of any concessions or inducements paid to put the lease in place (resultant net value is then converted to the equivalent level payment stream that would produce an equivalent net present value at that discount rate).

**escrow** Item of value, money, or documents deposited with a third party to be delivered upon the fulfillment of a condition; for example, the deposit by a borrower with the lender of funds to pay taxes and insurance premiums when they become due, or the deposit of funds or documents with an attorney or escrow agent to be disbursed upon the closing of a sale of real estate (in some parts of the country, escrows of taxes and insurance premiums are called *impounds* or *reserves*).

**escrow account** Segregated trust account in which escrow funds are held.

**escrow analysis** Periodic examination of escrow accounts to determine if current monthly deposits will provide sufficient funds to pay taxes, insurance, and other bills when due.

**escrow transfer agreement** Instrument transferring escrow funds (and obligations under an existing escrow agreement) held by the lender to a third party upon transfer of property.

**estoppel certificate** Written statement setting forth certain facts which cannot later be repudiated (frequently given by a lender or a tenant relative to a loan or lease, respectively).

**excess (positive) cash flow** Amount of income derived from the operation of a property or business after deducting or paying all expenses.

**excess coverage** Coverage designed to be in excess over one or more primary policies, which will not pay out until the primary limits of liability are exhausted.

**exclusive listing** Written contract giving one licensed real estate agent the exclusive right to sell a property for a specified time, but reserving the owner's right to sell the property alone without the payment of a commission.

**expense stop** *See* base stop.

**exposure** Total amount a lender has tied up in a loan; usually the outstanding principal balance of the loan plus accrued interest, and any capitalized costs including legal fees and expenses, appraisal and environmental fees, and all other costs associated with securing the lender's interest in the property.

**extended coverage** Common extension of coverage beyond the normal fire and lightning perils; damage caused by windstorm, hail, explosion, riot, vehicles, smoke, aircraft, and other falling objects are the additional perils insured by this coverage.

**fair market value** Price at which property is transferred between a willing buyer and a willing seller, each of whom has a reasonable knowledge of all pertinent facts and neither being under any compulsion to buy or sell.

**Fannie Mae (Federal National Mortgage Association)** Nation's largest mortgage investor created in 1968 by an amendment to Title III of the National Housing Act (12 USC 1716 et seq.); stockholder-owner corporation, a portion of whose board of directors is appointed by the President of the United States, supports the secondary market in mortgages on residential property with mortgage purchase and securitization programs.

**Fannie Mae DUS lender** Lender designated by Fannie Mae who originates, underwrites, closes, and services Fannie Mae approved multifamily mortgage loans.

**FDIC** *See* Federal Deposit Insurance Corporation.

**federal bank wire** Payment system operated by the Federal Reserve for the transfer of federal funds balances between financial institutions maintaining accounts at U.S. Federal Reserve Banks.

**Federal Deposit Insurance Corporation (FDIC)** Originally established by the Banking Act of 1933 to protect depositors from loss; as a result of the Financial Institutions Reform, Recovery and Enforcement Act of 1989 (FIRREA), the FDIC administers the Bank Insurance Fund (BIF), and the Savings Association Insurance Fund (SAIF).

**Federal Home Loan Mortgage Corporation** *See* Freddie Mac.

**Federal National Mortgage Association** *See* Fannie Mae.

**fee simple** Greatest possible interest a person can have in real estate, including the right to dispose of the property or pass it on to one's heirs.

**FHLMC (Federal Home Loan Mortgage Corporation)** *See* Freddie Mac.

**fidelity (bond)** Type of insurance that generally covers losses caused by dishonest or fraudulent acts by employees and others.

**final rule** Attempts to state the circumstances under which lenders would not be deemed "participating in the management" or "influencing" the control, handling, or disposal of hazardous materials at a borrower's property and, therefore, would not be liable for their remediation.

**financial statement** Financial report, including a balance sheet and an income statement.

**financing statement** Under the Uniform Commercial Code (UCC), a prescribed document a lender files with the Recorder of Deeds or Secretary of State, giving the name and address of the debtor and the secured party (lender), along with a description of the personal property securing the loan.

**financial statement analysis** Evaluation of the existing and potential income stream of the real estate to determine prospective cash flow and debt service capacity.

**first mortgage** Mortgage that gives the mortgagee a security right over all other mortgages of the mortgaged property.

**fixture** Personal property that becomes real property upon being attached to real estate.

**FNMA (Federal National Mortgage Association)** *See* Fannie Mae.

**flood insurance** Insurance that reimburses the policyholder for damage to property caused by the peril of flood.

**forbearance** Act of refraining from taking legal action despite the fact that the mortgage is in arrears; usually granted only when a mortgagor makes satisfactory arrangements to pay the amount owed at a future date.

**force majeure insurance** Specialized form of coverage for owners and contractors to protect against damage or delays caused by unpredictable events such as war, strikes, or those perils not normally insured under all risk policies.

**forced placed coverage** Hazard coverage obtained by a lender to protect its security interest in a property where the borrower has failed to renew existing coverage; premiums are usually above market rates and most mortgage instruments allow for this premium to be charged to the borrower.

**foreclosure** Legal procedure in which a mortgaged property is sold in a legal process to pay the outstanding debt in case of default.

**Freddie Mac (Federal Home Loan Mortgage Corporation)** Created by Congress in Title III of the Emergency Home Finance Act of 1970 (12 USC 1451 et seq.); stockholder-owned corporation, a portion of whose board of directors is appointed by the President of the United States, supports the secondary market in mortgages on residential and multifamily properties with mortgage purchase and securitization programs.

**friable** Condition, most frequently utilized in the context of asbestos, where environmental contaminants (usually asbestos fibers) have the potential to become dislodged or disturbed and airborne, thus becoming a threat to health.

**funding** Payment of loan money by a lender to a borrower so that he or she can purchase real estate, or the payment of money by investors to lenders in return for mortgages sold to them by the lender.

**generally accepted accounting principles (GAAP)** Accounting practices mandated by recognized rule-making authorities.

**general contractor** Party that performs or supervises the construction or development of a property pursuant to the terms of a primary contract with the owner; general contractor may use its own employees for this work or the services of other contractors (subcontractors).

**grace period** Period of time (usually measured in days) after an obligation is due or is to be performed during which a borrower can perform without incurring a penalty and without being considered in default.

**gross rate** Interest rate on a mortgage, including servicing fees.

**groundwater** Water in the subsoil.

**guarantee** Individual's or entity's promise to pay in the event of an operational shortfall.

**guarantor** Party secondarily liable for another's debt or performance (in contrast to a surety, who is primarily liable with the principal debtor).

**guaranty** Promise by one party to pay a debt or perform an obligation contracted for or by another in the event that the obligor fails to pay or perform as contracted.

**hazard insurance** Insurance coverage that provides compensation to the insured in case of property loss or damage.

**hazard waste risk** Financial or health risk created due to any substance such as asbestos, urea formaldehyde foam insulation, transformers containing excess PCBs, lead paint, or any substance deemed hazardous or toxic, or required to be disclosed, reported, treated, removed, disposed of, or cleaned up by any applicable hazardous material law.

**highest and best use** Use of land that will bring the greatest return.

**holdback** Portion of a loan commitment not funded until some additional requirement, such as rental or construction completion, is attained. In construction or interim lending, a percentage of the contractor's draw held back to provide additional protection for the interim lender, often an amount equal to the contractor's profit given over when the interim loan is closed.

**HVAC** Heating, ventilating, and air-conditioning system.

**hypothecate** To pledge property as security for a debt without giving up possession of title.

**income approach to value** Appraisal technique used to estimate real property value by capitalizing net income.

**income and expense statement** Actual or estimated schedule of income and expense items reflecting net gain or loss during a specified period.

**income approach to value** Appraisal technique used to estimate real property value by capitalizing net income.

**indemnify** To protect against damage, loss, or injury, or to make compensation to for damage, loss, or injury.

**indemnity** Security against or compensation for damage, loss, or injury; also, a legal exemption from liability for damages.

**index** Published interest rate, such as the prime rate, LIBOR, T-Bill rate, or the 11th District COFI; lenders use indexes to establish interest rates charged on mortgages or to compare investment returns; on ARMs, a predetermined margin is added to the index to compute the interest rate adjustment.

**inflation guard** Endorsement to an insurance policy that increases coverage to offset the effects of inflation.

**infrastructure** Basic public improvements such as roads, sewers, water, drainage, and other utilities that are necessary to prepare raw land for buildings and future development.

**ingress** To go in; used with *egress* (to go out) to describe the right of access to land.

**innocent landowner defense** Term utilized by an owner of property, including a mortgagee who has taken title to property by judicial proceeding or by deed-in-lieu of foreclosure, in the context of avoiding liability for environmental contamination where the owner has taken certain precautions to ascertain the environmental condition of property prior to acquiring the property.

**installment** Periodic payment that a borrower agrees to pay a mortgage lender.

**insurance vacancy clause** Provision in a hazard insurance policy protecting the insured upon the occurrence of property loss or damage, even if the insured property is vacant (for an extended period of time).

**insured** Term preferred over other terms such as "policyholder" or "policyowner," to describe the party protected under an insurance contract to whom the insurer reimburses losses, pays benefits, or provides services.

**intangible property** Generally, property that has no intrinsic or marketable value in and of itself, but is merely the evidence of value, such as promissory notes, stock certificates, or certificates of deposits (as distinguished from land, furniture, and equipment).

**interest reserve** Holdback of loan proceeds by a lender to be utilized to pay interest as it accrues on a loan.

**interest** Consideration in the form of money paid for the use of money, usually expressed as an annual percentage; also, a "right, share, or title in property."

**interest rate** Percentage paid for the use of money, usually expressed as an annual percentage.

**joint and several note** Two or more persons or entities, each of whom is liable for the full amount of the debt.

**judgment** Final determination by a court of the rights and claims of the parties to an action.

**junior lenders (mortgage)** A mortgage that is subordinate to the claims of a prior lien or mortgage.

**landlord** Owner or lessor of real property.

**late charge** Additional charge that a borrower is required to pay as a penalty for failure to pay a regular installment when due.

**lease analysis** Formal review of a lease that is usually memorialized in writing on a form that provides details of the business terms and legal issues.

**lease audit** Official examination and verification of the status of leases (or a lease) to prove or ascertain the lease terms and their adequacy.

**lease guaranty** Instrument by which an individual or entity guaranties payment and/or performance of the tenant's obligations under the tenant's lease.

**lease concessions** Grant/concession given by a landlord to a tenant to induce the tenant to execute a lease (i.e., period of free or reduced rent or improving the leased premise at the landlord's expense).

**lease** Written document containing the conditions under which the possession and use of real and/or personal property are given by the owner to another for a stated period and consideration.

**lease modification** Instrument modifying the original lease and its terms and conditions.

**lease summary abstract** Brief lease analysis (on a legal basis) which can be recorded.

**legal description** Property description, recognized by law, that is sufficient to locate and identify the property without oral testimony.

**lender** Person or entity that invests in or originates loans, such as a mortgage banker, credit union, commercial bank, or savings and loan; in commercial property usage, the lender may be a life insurance company, bank, or pension fund that provides the funds and in whose name the loan is closed.

**lender liability** Area of legal findings that would hold the lender financially responsible for damages and costs based upon the lender's activities (especially in the management of real estate securing any of the lender's mortgage loans as this relates to environmental clean-up liability).

**lessee** One holding right of possession and use of property under the terms of a lease; also, "tenant."

**lessor** One who leases property to a lessee; also, "landlord."

**letter of attornment** *See* attornment agreement.

**letter of credit** Letter authorizing a person or company to draw on a bank, or stating that the bank will honor their credit up to the stated amount.

**liability** Accounting term signifying money owed or expected to be owed to another party; in law, a legal term signifying a legal obligation.

**liability insurance** Insurance covering the risks related to the property and personal liability claims of other parties against the insured party.

**liberalization clause** Clause in policies which states that if policies or endorsements currently in force are broadened by the passage of legislation or rulings from rating bodies, such policies or endorsements will be construed to include the broadening features.

**license** Generally, permission by a lawful authority to do an act which, without such permission, would be illegal; in real property, a privilege to enter for a specified purpose (for example, to collect rents), but does not confer on, or vest in, the licensee any title or estate in the property.

**lien** Legal hold or claim of a creditor on the property of another as security for a debt; may be against real or personal property.

**lien waiver** Waiver of mechanic's lien rights; a document signed by a supplier or subcontractor stating that the firm has been compensated for its work, thereby giving up its right to file a claim against the property.

**liquidation value** Value of an asset upon its sale or disposition.

**listing** Written authorization for an agent to sell or lease real estate.

**loan-to-value ratio (LTV)** Ratio of amount borrowed to appraised value or sales price of real property expressed as a percentage.

**loan transfer** Assumption of existing financing by a new owner when a property is sold.

**lockbox** Postal address, maintained by the firm's bank, that is used solely for the purpose of collecting checks; major goal is to reduce collection float, because the receipts are immediately credited to the firm's bank account.

**loss draft** Insurance payments in settlement of a claim for damage to mortgaged property; generally made out to both the mortgagee and mortgagor.

**loss of rents coverage** *See* Rental income insurance.

**loss payable clause** Insurance policy provision for the payment of a claim to someone other than the insured, who holds an insurable interest in the insured property.

**loss payee** Party named in a loss payable clause to whom insurance proceeds are to be paid in the event of damage to property in which the loss payee has an insurable interest; include automobile lien holders and property mortgagees.

**major tenants** In commercial property, firms that are key lessees/tenants because of their high credit standing, the amount of space they occupy, and/or the percentage of gross rent they pay.

**market** Current supply and demand characteristics of a commodity in a given geographic/economic setting.

**market approach to value** In an appraisal, a market value estimate of the property based on actual prices paid in similar market transactions.

**market rent** Price a tenant pays a landlord for the use and occupancy of real property based on current rent for comparable property.

**marketable title** A title that may not be completely clear, but has only minor objections that a well-informed and prudent buyer of real estate would accept.

**market value** Highest price that a buyer and the lowest price that a seller would accept, neither one being compelled to buy or sell; also, "fair market value."

**master lease** Lease under which the leasehold is further subleased by the tenant to one or more subtenants.

**maturity** Date on which an agreement expires; termination of a promissory note.

**mechanic's lien** Claim created by law to secure priority of payment for work performed and materials provided by a vendor; land may be liened, as well as buildings, equipment, or other property.

**menu pricing** Method of service fee calculation where each function the servicer performs for the lender has a corresponding fee.

**menu pricing fee** Generally expressed in basis points ("bp") and calculated using the loan balance.

**MIP ( Mortgage insurance premium)** Amount paid by a mortgagor for mortgage insurance either to FHA or a private mortgage insurance company.

**monetary default** Breach or nonperformance of the terms of the note due to the nonpayment of debt service or escrow payments.

**moratorium** Legal authorization to delay the enforcement of liability for debt, or to suspend an activity.

**mortgage** Pledge of property, usually real property, as security for a debt; by extension, the document evidencing the pledge; document may contain the terms of repayment of the debt; by further extension, mortgage may be used to describe both the mortgage proper and the separate promissory note evidencing the debt and providing the terms of the debt's repayment (in many states this document is a deed of trust).

**mortgagee clause** Clause attached to an insurance policy stipulating that the lender is to receive insurance proceeds sufficient to satisfy the unpaid amount of a loan.

**mortgagee** Lender in a mortgage transaction.

**mortgagee in possession** Mortgagee who, due to default under the terms of a mortgage, has obtained possession but not ownership of the property.

**MSA (metropolitan statistical area)** Geographic area designated by the U.S. Census Bureau for purposes of collecting and disseminating demographic information.

**NAIC (National Association of Insurance Commissioners)** Organization whose membership consists of state insurance regulators and whose objectives are to promote uniformity in regulation by drafting model laws and regulations for adoption by the states and to provide support services to insurance departments such as examinations and statistical information.

**named insured** Individual, business, or organization specified in the declarations by name as the insured(s) under a policy.

**named perils** Policy that specifically lists the perils insured against, as opposed to an *all risk* policy that covers all perils other than those specifically excluded.

**negative cash flow** Deficit created when expenditures required to maintain an investment exceed income received on the property.

**negotiable instrument** Written order to pay, such as a check or promissory note, that may be transferred from one person to another provided certain conditions are met.

**net effective rent** Rental income generated by a lease computed over the life of the lease after deduction of total rent concessions and expressed as an annual dollar amount or annual dollar amount per square foot.

**net rate** Rate of interest remitted to an investor after servicing fees have been deducted from the gross rate.

**net operating income (NOI)** Amount remaining after total operating expenses (excluding interest payments) are deducted from effective gross income.

**net realizable value** Amount or figure resulting from the sale or disposition of property or an asset after all expenses associated with such sale or disposition are paid.

**net rentable area** Actual square footage of a building that can be rented (common areas, such as hallways, lobbies, elevator shafts, etc., are generally not included).

**net worth** Value of all assets, including cash, less total liabilities; often used as an underwriting guideline to indicate creditworthiness and financial strength.

**non-disturbance agreement** Agreement that permits a tenant under a lease to remain in possession despite any foreclosure.

**non-monetary default** Breach or nonperformance of any of the terms or covenants of the loan documents other than debt service and escrow payments.

**non-performing loan** Loan that has not fulfilled one or more of the terms, covenants, conditions, or obligations required under the mortgage.

**nonrecourse loan** Type of loan that prohibits the lender from attempting to recover against the borrower (personally) if the security value for the loan falls below the amount required to repay the loan.

**non-waiver provision** Provision reserving to a lender every right under a document or at law not previously waived (note: a general term for any kind of paper or document signed by a borrower that is an acknowledgment of the debt, and is, by inference, a promise to pay; when the note is secured by a mortgage, it is called a mortgage note and the mortgagee is named as the payee).

**occurrence** Accident, including continuous or repeated exposure, that results in bodily injury or property damage neither expected or intended by the insured; occurrence policies cover claims that occur during the policy period regardless of when the claim is made against the policy; *See* claims made.

**occupancy rate** Percentage of space or units that are leased or occupied.

**open listing** Written contract that does not allow one licensed real estate agent the exclusive right to sell a property for a specified time, but reserving the owner's right to sell the property alone without the payment of a commission.

**open period** Interval of time under a mortgage during which the loan can be prepaid.

**operating statement** *See* income and expense statement.

**operations and maintenance plan** Plan adopted for maintaining and remediating a known or potential environmental condition, usually utilized in the context of asbestos contamination.

**opinion letter** Letter issued by an attorney containing legal opinions addressing a variety of legal issues.

**partial payment** Payment of only a portion of the required amount due including payments received without the late charge.

**partial release** Instrument discharging only a portion of the secured property from a lien.

**partnership agreement** Contract between a business association of two or more owners who share in the profits and losses of the business.

**payment and performance bonds** Bond to guarantee payment/performance of certain specified acts, such as the completion of construction of a property or the payment/cost thereof.

**payoff letter** Statement detailing the unpaid principal balance, accrued interest, outstanding late charges, legal fees, and all other amounts necessary to pay off the lender in full.

**percentage rent** Rent, computed as a percentage of retail sales above a breakpoint, paid by tenants under typical retail leases; usually paid instead of or in addition to a specified minimum base rent.

**perfection** Perfection is frequently used in the context of a security interest, and it means those steps legally required to give a secured party an interest in property against a debtor's creditors.

**performing loan** Loan that has and continues to fulfill all of the terms, covenants, conditions, or obligations required under the mortgage.

**personal injury** Injury other than those arising out of bodily injury, such as false arrest, malicious prosecution, wrongful entry, or eviction, libel, or slander, or violation of privacy; extent of such coverage may vary from policy to policy.

**personal property** Any property that is not real property; also, "chattel."

**Phase I Environmental Audit** Basic study conducted to evaluate the environmental condition of real property and/or improvements.

**Phase II Environmental Audit** Study of the environmental condition of property/improvements that is more detailed and in-depth than a Phase I audit; may include groundwater testing or testing of soil.

**plans and specifications** Architectural and engineering drawings and specifications for construction of a building or project; include a description of materials to be used and the manner in which they are to be applied.

**pledge agreement** Instrument pursuant to which a borrower will assign/pledge as collateral for a loan a security interest in certain types of property (e.g., stock, accounts, etc.).

**plot plan** Layout of improvements on a site, including their location, dimensions, and landscapes; generally a part of the architectural plan.

**policyholder surplus** Amount by which an insurance company's assets exceed its liabilities, as reported in its annual statement; for a stock insurer the policyholder surplus would be the sum of its capital and surplus; for a mutual insurer, the policyholder surplus equals the company's surplus.

**portfolio** Collection of loans held for servicing or investment.

**power of sale** Provision in a deed of trust or mortgage that empowers a trustee, without court order, to sell property in the event of default by the mortgagor and to apply the proceeds of the sale to satisfy the obligation, the costs of invoking the procedure, and the expenses of the sale.

**premium** Amount paid, often in addition to the interest, to secure a loan.

**prepayment** Payment of all or part of a mortgage debt before it is due.

**prepayment penalty/premium** Charge the mortgagor pays the mortgagee for the privilege to prepay the loan.

**prepayment privilege** Right given a borrower in the mortgage to pay all or part of a mortgage debt without penalty prior to its maturity.

**present value** Current value of cash received at a definite point or points in the future.

**principal** Original balance of money lent, excluding interest; also, the remaining balance of a loan, excluding interest.

**priority** Order of precedence of liens against property or assets; usually established by filing or recordation of liens, but may be established by statute or agreement.

**promissory note** Written promise to pay a specific amount at a specified time.

**proof of loss** Formal statement by an insured to his insurer outlining the circumstances of a loss and the amount of damage being sought in compensation.

**property inspection** Physical review/evaluation of a property to determine its current structural condition, to report any deferred maintenance and/or environmental problems, and to verify leasing status.

**property manager** Individual or company responsible for the daily and long range management of the operations of a property.

**purchase agreement** Written agreement between a buyer and seller of real property, setting forth the price and terms of the sale.

**real estate** *See* real property.

**real property** Land and improvements permanently attached to it, such as buildings; in some states, this term is synonymous with the term *real estate.*

**receiver** Impartial person appointed by the court to administer properties involved in foreclosure or other litigation, to receive its rents and profits, and to apply or dispose of them at the direction of the court.

**recourse loan** Type of mortgage loan in which the lender's remedies in the event of borrower default are unlimited, extending beyond the property to the borrower's personal assets; in secondary marketing, loan that the lender must repurchase in the case of loan default or other defect.

**redemption period** Time allowed by law in some states during which mortgagors may buy back their foreclosed properties by paying the balance owed on their delinquent mortgages, plus interest and fees.

**red flag** Warning term used to indicate further analysis is warranted.

**refinancing** Repayment of a debt from the proceeds of a new loan, using the same property as security.

**regulatory agency** Arm of the state or federal government that has the responsibility to license, pass laws, regulate, audit, and monitor industry related issues (i.e., NAIC, FHLBB, HUD).

**reinsurance** The practice of one insurance company (the reinsured) accepting risks or business from another insurer (the ceding company); allows insurers to maintain a larger spread of risk and avoid large catastrophes.

**release** Discharging of secured property from a lien.

**remediation** Process by which contaminants are removed from a building or site.

**remedy** Means by which a right is enforced or the violation of a right is prevented, redressed, or compensated.

**remittance report** Report detailing the respective funds sent to the lender.

**rent roll** List of tenants leasing a property; it details terms of lease, area leased, and the amount of rent being paid.

**rentable area** Area of a property, measured in square feet, upon which rent can be collected.

**rental concession** Landlord's agreement to forgo part of the advertised rent in an effort to attract tenants.

**rental income insurance** Form of property insurance that pays the owner of a building (or other designated loss payee) for the amount of rent lost due to damage from an insured peril; also, "loss of rents coverage."

**replacement cost** Cost to replace a structure with one of equivalent value and function, but not necessarily identical in design or materials.

**replacement cost endorsement** Insurance endorsement used with a policy to insure that coverage is on a replacement cost basis.

**replacement reserve** Cash reserve for the replacement of fixed assets.

**reserves** Funded or non-funded accounts set up at either the property or portfolio level in anticipation of periodic or non-periodic capital expenditures or cash needs.

**restructure** Loan for which the basic terms, such as interest rate, maturity date, collateral, or guaranty have been modified as a result of actual or anticipated delinquency; also, a "workout."

**retainage (retention)** Amount of payments withheld from contractors or subcontractors per contractual agreement to insure final and satisfactory completion of job.

**satisfaction** Discharge of an obligation by paying a party what it is due.

**satisfaction of mortgage** Recorded instrument the lender provides to evidence payment in full of the mortgage debt.

**scope of work** Description of the nature of service, activities, studies, jobs, or work to be undertaken by a party.

**secondary financing** Funding method using a loan secured by a second mortgage on a property; sometimes used to refer to any financing technique other than equity and first mortgage debt.

**secondary mortgage market** Market where lenders and investors buy and sell existing mortgages or mortgage-backed securities, thereby providing greater availability of funds for additional mortgage lending.

**security deposit** Deposit of money by a tenant to a landlord to secure performance of a written or oral rental agreement (lease).

**security document/instrument** Mortgage, or deed of trust, evidencing the pledge of real estate as collateral for the loan.

**security interest** Interest of a creditor in the security collateralizing an investment.

**sequester of rents** Court-related action by which rental income derived from property is ordered by the court to be deposited with and held by the clerk of the court or other governmental/court official.

**servicing fee/rate** Fee earned by a servicer for administering a loan for an investor usually expressed as a percentage of the unpaid principal balance of the loan and deducted from the monthly mortgage payment.

**servicing spread** That portion of the interest rate added by the lender to cover the cost of administering the mortgage asset.

**setback lines** Lines that define the required distances for the location of a structure in relation to the perimeter of the property; in accordance with building codes, deed restrictions, and zoning requirements.

**settlement statement** *See* closing statement.

**site plan** Drawing that shows all improvements to a site, such as clearing, grading, and the installation of public utilities, before the actual construction of a building.

**stabilization** Measurement over a period of time to establish an average or expected outcome.

**subcontractor** Person or company contracted to perform work for a developer or general contractor.

**subdivision** Improved or unimproved land divided into a number of parcels for sale, lease, financing, or development.

**sublease** Lease executed by a lessee to a third person for a term no longer than the remaining portion of the original lease.

**subordinate lien** Lien or encumbrance (for example, a second mortgage or mechanic's lien) on real estate whose priority is inferior to another's recorded interest in the same property.

**subordination agreement** Document by which parties acknowledge, by written record, that the debt of one is inferior to the debt or interest of another in the same property; may apply not only to mortgages, but also to leases, real estate rights, and any other types of debt interests.

**subordination (lease) provision** Clause in a lease by which the tenant acknowledges that its interest in the lease premises is inferior to the interest of the lender whose mortgage encumbers the leased premises.

**subrogation** Right of a party to proceed against another for recovery.

**super priority lien** Lien or encumbrance on property that is superior to most every other claim against the same property irrespective of the time of recording or claiming the lien or encumbrance (usually arising in the context of liens for remediating hazardous waste).

**superior lien** Lien or encumbrance (for example, a mortgage or mechanic's lien) on real estate whose priority is greater (or superior) to the interest of another's interest in the same property.

**survey** Measurement of land, prepared by a registered land surveyor, showing the location of the land with reference to known points, its dimensions, and the location and dimensions of any improvements.

**surveyor's certificate** Formal statement, signed, certified, and dated by a surveyor giving the pertinent facts about a particular property and any easements or encroachments affecting it.

**tenant** One who is not the owner but occupies real property under consent of the owner and in subordination to the owner's title; entitled to exclusive possession, use, and enjoyment of the property, usually for a time and amount specified in the lease.

**tenant improvements** Constructed improvements to the base building, such as interior partitions, drop ceilings, and other finishes that prepare a space for occupancy and use by a tenant.

**term** Period of time between the commencement date and termination date of a note, mortgage, legal document, or other contract.

**third party** One not a party to an agreement or a transaction, but who may have rights therein.

**title binder** Written evidence of temporary title insurance coverage that runs for a limited time and must be replaced by a permanent policy.

**title exception** Exclusion appearing in a title insurance policy against which the insurance company does not insure.

**title insurance commitment** *See* title binder.

**title insurance policy** Contract by which the insurer agrees to pay the insured a specific amount for any loss caused by defects of title to real estate, wherein the insured has an interest as purchaser, mortgagee, or otherwise.

**title search** Examination of public records, laws, and court decisions to ensure that no one except the seller has a valid claim to the property and to disclose past and current facts regarding ownership of the subject property.

**title update** Examination of public records from the date of a previous title search to ascertain the status of title to property since such last search.

**transfer** *See* assumption.

**transfer fees** Fees charged by an investor or servicer to process a transfer of ownership request.

**umbrella insurance** Type of policy obtained by an insured to cover loss or damage for a number of properties or other assets, or a number of companies (such as subsidiaries of a parent company).

**underwriting criteria** In mortgage banking, the analysis of the risk involved in making a mortgage loan to determine whether the risk is acceptable to the lender; involves the evaluation of the property as outlined in the appraisal report, and of the borrower's ability and willingness to repay the loan.

**Uniform Commercial Code (UCC)** Comprehensive code of laws regulating important legal aspects of business and financial transactions; accepted by every state except Louisiana.

**usable area** Actual number of square feet contained within a tenant's demised space.

**usury** Act of charging borrowers a rate of interest greater than that permitted by law.

**usury saving clause** Clause in a loan document intended to protect the lender from a claim that an unlawful amount of interest is being charged.

**utilities** Basic services associated with developed areas that include provisions for electricity, telephone, gas, water, and garbage collection.

**voluntary petition of bankruptcy** Voluntary action filed under the United States Bankruptcy Code (the "Code") by a debtor seeking protection under the Code.

**waiver of subrogation** Endorsement issued by an insurer that waives its right of subrogation against a third party; usually requested by an insured in conjunction with a lease.

**waiver of trial by jury provision** Provision in a loan document whereby the borrower and/or lender waive their respective rights to a trial by jury in a legal action/lawsuit on a loan document.

**waste** Abuse or destructive use of property by one in rightful possession (such as an owner or tenant).

**watchlist** List of loans which, while current in terms of monthly payments, pose a potential risk of loss due to deferred maintenance, delinquent real estate taxes, low debt service coverage, major lease expirations, or other signs of increasing financial stress on property performance.

**working files** Files used to store correspondence, insurance, and tax information, mortgage document copies, and any other information used in the day-to-day servicing of a mortgage loan; also commonly referred to as "servicing files."

**workout** Alternative action to foreclosure for the benefit of the lender and the borrower; includes loan modification, short sales, and various forms of forbearance; also, "restructure."

**yield maintenance** Prepayment premium that will equal the present value of any costs to the lender resulting from the difference in interest rates between the date of the note and the date on which the prepayment is made.

**zoning** Creation of districts by local governments in which specific types of property uses are authorized.